Praise for

"With his practical coaching cap on, Tommy masterfully shares how men can achieve something of ultra-significance—*Winning Character*. It's a rare kind of character that can be used greatly by God for good."

—Mark W. Merrill, president, Family First

"Every one wants to be a person of real influence, and Tommy Bowden clearly shows us how in *Winning Character*. Through solid biblical examples and his own personal lessons learned from a lifetime in football, he describes the essential elements needed to become a man of genuine, godly influence. Written in a casual, conversational style, every man will want this book that clearly demonstrates how the key ingredient for success in any field is always character. I recommend it highly."

—Les Steckel, veteran NFL coach and president, Fellowship of Christian Athletes

"In so many ways sports mirrors life and no sport perhaps so much as college football. Tommy Bowden gives an inside look as to why character is so important both on and off the field that is fascinating, inspiring, and engaging from the first word to the last. A great read from a great man from a great family."

—James Merritt, senior pastor, Cross Pointe Church in Duluth, Georgia, and host of Touching Lives international broadcast ministries

"From the penthouse to the outhouse . . . that experience can reveal the person within. Coach Bowden shares his life story in a transparent honesty that is riveting and inspiring. In the words of his father, 'It's dadgum good.'"

—**Jim Henry**, pastor emeritus, First Baptist Church, Orlando, Florida

"I remember someone once telling me that football doesn't build character, it reveals it. I thought of that as I read Tommy Bowden's book *Winning Character*. The Bowdens are a credit to the game of college football, and Tommy does an excellent job of showing us how work and faith are interwoven in his life and in the lives of his wonderful family. It is a great road map for any of us."

—**Mac Brown**, head football coach, University of Texas

"Our country is desperate for men who have a kingdom understanding, perspective, and vision. Tommy Bowden set a foundation in his life and leadership that led to a championship run that cannot be measured by mortal man. Cut from undoubtedly the most storied coaching family in the history of college football, it is no mere coincidence that the most important thing in his life was NOT football. *Winning Character* is a championship game plan written by a kingdom man with a kingdom agenda! Coach Bowden is no longer on the sideline, but he is still chasing a championship. This trophy will be placed on his head, not in his hands . . . and it is the one that matters!"

—**Dr. Tony Evans**, senior pastor, Oak Cliff Bible Fellowship and author of *Kingdom Man*

"Tommy Bowden is a maker of men out of boys. All dads, pastors, mentors, and men who care about reducing suffering and creating health in their personal world and spheres of influence need to devour the simplicity and power of this book! Thank you, Coach, for being intentional in the lives of the men you lead and for giving us a path to mentor men that is so impactful."

—**Kenny Luck**, men's pastor, Saddleback Church, founder and president of Every Man Ministries, and author of *Sleeping Giant*

"If you want to learn about winning, look at and listen to a winner! Coach Tommy Bowden's new book *Winning Character* explains in his characteristic, no nonsense style the nonnegotiables for winning in every area of life. This book is a must-read for every man who wants to succeed in his family, career, and relationship with God."

—**Dr. Robert Jeffress**, pastor, First Baptist Church, Dallas, Texas

"Coach Tommy Bowden has been a successful football coach at the highest levels. He has been a mentor and role model to all his players, coaches, community where he lives, and in the public eye. He has shared these critical points of character, accountability, responsibility, discipline, and sacrifice with us in his book *Winning Character*. In the day and age where we in the ministry want to keep our ministry in the headlines and us out of them, Coach Bowden outlines the biblical principles that are nonnegotiable in winning at life. This is an excellent study for a gathering of men sharing life together."

—**Darrel Billups**, executive director, National Coalition of Ministry to Men (NCMM)

"With so many books out there about winning at life, it is refreshing to have someone like Coach Tommy Bowden share his life's experiences. He has led literally thousands of men with successful results. Coach Bowden has lived out the principles in this book, and these biblical foundations have been a bedrock in his personal and very visible professional career. Most of us guys who have been involved in sports and have witnessed the whole Bowden clan for all these years can now read the real reason for their successes both on and off the field. A must read for any guy who wants to be a better man, husband, and dad."

—**John Croyle**, former All-American football player, University of Alabama and founder of Big Oak Ranch | A Christian Home for Children Needing a Chance

WINNING
CHARACTER

WINNING
CHARACTER

A PROVEN GAME PLAN FOR SUCCESS

TOMMY
BOWDEN

WITH LAWRENCE KIMBROUGH

B&H
PUBLISHING GROUP

NASHVILLE, TENNESSEE

978-1-4336-7860-8

Published by B&H Publishing Group

Nashville, Tennessee

Dewey Decimal Classification: 248.842

Subject Heading: MEN \ CHARACTER \
CHRISTIAN LIFE

1 2 3 4 5 6 7 8 • 16 15 14 13 12

Contents

I dedicate this book to my wife Linda, children Ryan and Lauren, and my parents, Bobby and Ann Bowden. With the pressures of a secular world making following God's will more and more difficult, a Godly family core is essential. I love you all."

Acknowledgments

It took a winning team to make this book a reality! Thanks to Thom Rainer, Bruce Raley, and the LifeWay team for believing in me and in my message. Thanks to Lawrence Kimbrough, Selma Wilson, Jedidiah Coppenger, and B&H Publishing Group for putting my thoughts and words into these pages. Thanks to Jason Ellerbrook, Darilynn Keith, and all involved in LifeWay Men for casting the vision for this book and dreaming ways that we can impact men together through the platform God gave me! Finally, a special thanks to all of the players, coaches, and college football teams I had the honor of working with over the past thirty-two years. Together we drew the line between character and compromise and we won a bunch of games along the way!

Foreword

I would love to tell you a little bit about my second son, Tommy Bowden. He is a natural born leader. He is the third child of six and was born in Birmingham, Alabama, while I was coaching football at Howard College, now named Samford University, in 1954. At the age of two, we moved to Douglas, Georgia, where Tommy eventually entered grammar school. We later moved to West Virginia where Tommy graduated from Morgantown High School. He attended West Virginia University where he received a football scholarship. And Tommy was not just on the roster; he started as a flankerback in the West Virginia victory over North Carolina State in the 1975 Peach Bowl.

While growing up, Tommy never gave his mother or me any problems. His life always manifested strong character traits, regardless of the situation. Tommy's early life was also marked by a great love for football. In a term paper he wrote while attending Morgantown High School, Tommy stated his desire to be a football coach like me. After graduating from West Virginia in 1976, he took a coaching position with me at Florida State. We had a great time. His coaching gifts and commitment eventually led him, after the 1982 season, to accept his first full-time assistant coaching role at East Carolina University. Like me, he began moving his family to a number of different schools. In the following years, he took similar positions in schools such as Duke, Alabama, Kentucky, and Auburn. After this, Tommy took his first head coaching job at Tulane University. Tommy's love for football and strong character enabled him to revive Tulane's program, leading them to an undefeated season. Not long after that, Tommy accepted the head coaching job at Clemson University, serving nine strong years before retiring from coaching.

If you really want to understand Tommy, you have to understand his great love for Jesus and the Bible. I really believe Tommy's strength comes from his diligent Bible study and prayer life with his wife, Linda. Tommy believes that Jesus is worthy of our trust and that the Scriptures are absolutely true. I've never seen him waver as he talks the talk and walks the walk! He is never shy about expressing his faith publicly. Tommy now speaks all over the USA to various Christian organizations and athletic groups. What you see is what you get! When Tommy was a head coach, he always had a full time chaplain for his team. He wanted all his players to know about our Savior before they graduated. He simply presented the gospel to them, like a professor does his students, and left it up to them whether or not they accepted it. He played his best players, regardless of their beliefs. There was team prayer before and after games. When Clemson and Florida State played in the first game ever in Division IA Football between a father and son in 1999, we had an FCA breakfast before the game in front of 1,000 fans. Tommy and I gave our testimonies. It became and annual affair every time we played in Clemson. I can't tell you how many times after Tommy spoke to religious organizations that many young people surrendered their life to Christ. His message is very clear and simple where all can understand it. Tommy loves Jesus and he wants others to hear the good news about Jesus.

In this book Tommy talks about our "power to influence." We must realize that our actions speak louder than our words. And our actions are a reflection of our character. The Scriptures are clear: We are to have Christ-like character. Unfortunately, we have all failed to reflect Christ-like character. But, thankfully, Christ lived the life we were all supposed to live and died the death we all deserved to die. By repenting of our sinful ways and trusting Jesus, God will accept us and see us as people who have Christ-like character. By God's grace, God uses our circumstances to shape us into people of character. Unfortunately, we all have a long way to go. *Winning Character* is just the kind of book we all need to hear in order to develop Christ-like character. I'm so proud of Tommy's work in this book. Hope you enjoy it as much as I did.

—Bobby Bowden

The Need to Win

Every coach loves second-and-short. He'll take all of those he can get.

I'll bet you would too.

But unfortunately, most days aren't second-and-short, are they? Most days don't come with that much room for error, where almost anything you decide to run will work—and where even if it doesn't, you're still likely to have another crack or two at a first down from close range.

Second-and-short just doesn't require nearly as tight of a game plan. It's a lot more wide-open.

Life, however, (much like football) is more second-and-nine, third-and-long—the occasional fourth-and-goal thrown in to really challenge you. And so winning decisions usually take a high level of effort and forethought. Everything needs to come together. Right play call. Good reads. Clear antici-pation of what the defense will be bringing. Followed by the pinpoint execution to carry it through. You don't want to leave it up to your quarterback to go create something out of nothing all the time. Nice when it happens, but it's not a high percentage play. Scrambling is not a success strategy.

Not when you're trying to convert on the all too frequent third-and-longs of real life.

But I talk to enough people—and I've lived enough years myself—to know there's a lot of scrambling going on these days. A lot of making things up as we go along. Improvising on the fly. And when that doesn't work, just punting the ball away. Just forget it. Not sure what else to do with a life where the clock is always running down on you, and always asking for more yardage than you think you can pick up.

Life's hard. I know that. Let's just say it that way. *Hard.* I know the opposition is tough. And I know how it feels to be scrambling, wishing you only needed a short gain but know-ing you've got a lot of ground to cover if you want to keep your drive going.

Thankfully, however, God has provided us a more prom-ising alternative. A more balanced attack at life. He has given us the option of living with *character.* And if we'll take it—and really live it—we'll end up doing a lot less scrambling and a lot more moving the ball down the field. Instead of running around without a plan or a playbook, we'll know where we're trying to go and how we intend to get there. With strength, resolve, and self-control.

I'd like to say that I've arrived at this conclusion by piling up one personal success on top of another. Truth is, that hasn't always been the case. Mine has not been a flawless run. The last thing I want to do is give the impression that I've handled everything in my life without a hitch, that if people would just watch and observe, they could see how things are supposed to be done. I assure you, I don't feel that way at all.

But even though acknowledging and confessing our own failures is certainly a healthy part of humility, I can't help thinking that if all we ever feel comfortable talking about is how far we keep missing the mark, then none of us can ever benefit from one another's successes. I mean, I know we usually learn the most valuable lessons in life from our mistakes. I've sure learned a whole lot from mine—and I've given myself plenty of material to work with. But if we don't ever talk about how God has helped us legitimately apply His Word in tangible, trusting, intentional ways to the challenges of everyday life, all we'll ever do is confirm to one another what a big bunch of losers we are.

I just think it calls for a little balance here.

I'm glad to be able to say, thanks to the power of God and a strong family heritage of faith and faithfulness, He has enabled me to employ some character traits in life that prove His Word positively true. I have seriously attempted—the best

I know how—to live with sincere obedience to Him. And by His grace He has blessed me in more ways than I can count.

Again, it's not because I'm perfect. And it's all for His glory, not mine. But as imperfect as this messenger is, the message itself is still true and right. I'm not the publisher of His Word, but I do want to be a good newspaper boy who delivers it with as much confidence and encouragement as I can give.

So I hope you understand where I'm coming from. I'm not trying to brag. I know that when a guy puts his thoughts and ideas into a book, people think he must know everything. That's obviously not the case here. A lot of things in my life are still in process. I readily admit that.

But I do want to show you what I've seen work with my family, my children, my ball teams, and the many other opportunities God has given me to impact people's lives. My goal is not to look better in print than I do in person. But I do hope that what you read in this book will give you a new hunger—along *with* me—for gaining the kind of character that can reorient your life in a more confident, deliberate direction.

Because that's what we need.

And one thing I know: we can trust God to give us what we need.

Back in October 1999—in the first of what immediately came to be known as the Bowden Bowl series—my father's

Florida State team came into Clemson undefeated and ranked #1 in the country. The media, of course, made a huge deal out of it. No father and son had ever coached against each other in a major college football game. We had so many interview requests come in that we had to start conducting them two weeks ahead—prior to our game with the previous week's opponent. Unheard of.

But take all the family context and carnival atmosphere out of it, and I'll just tell you—I wanted to win. *Bad.* It was my first year as head coach at Clemson. We were playing the #1 team in the nation. That victory alone would've put a real feather in my cap. And I wanted it. Prayed for it. Thought we had it, too, when we went up 14–3 at halftime.

But maybe God knew that wasn't what I really needed. Imagine a guy like me, fresh off an undefeated season the year before at Tulane University, taking down a huge opponent like that in my inaugural season at Clemson. Making a big statement on a national stage. Wow. I might've really thought I'd arrived, like I was the hottest commodity ever to hit the coaching ranks. I might never again have found a pillow ample enough to hold up that big head of mine. Maybe my heart just wasn't truly ready for that kind of immediate success. I don't know.

My father, on the other hand, *needed* this win. Ours was the first of three road games on their schedule for the last four weeks of the season, including their traditional finale against then-#4 Florida. And his 17–14 come-from-behind victory over us at Clemson (the three hundredth win of his career, by the way) kept alive his second and ultimately final national championship at Florida State. It was a legacy moment. And God was faithful to give it to him.

Fast-forward, now, to 2003—Bowden Bowl V—when things were a little bit different. My father came in at 8–1, having lost only to #2 Miami about a month before. He obviously wanted to win. Probably would've kept them in the national title hunt, even with one loss.

But that particular year, I *needed* to win. We had lost bad to Georgia on opening weekend. We had lost bad again at Maryland, then at North Carolina State. The week before, we had been trounced at home by Wake Forest 45–17. Fans booed us off the field. A loss to Florida State at that point in my career might have been curtains for me, despite the fact they were #3 in the nation at the time.

As it turned out, however, we pulled off the victory 26–10 in a stellar, inspired, knockout performance. And by the time we'd run through our last two opponents by huge margins to close out the season, followed by a 27–14 win over Tennessee in the Peach Bowl, I actually received—not my walking papers—but a three-year contract extension.

I *needed* that win.

God knows what we need.

He knows we need character.

And so when we come to Him on our third-and-long days, asking for His help in giving us courage, confidence, and perseverance for managing our various responsibilities, He will give it to us if we'll take it. Because we need it. And He knows it.

I've chosen to frame the two parts of this book by looking first at *foundations* and then finally at the *building blocks* of character. This idea has really come home to me in the last few months while we've been building our new house down here in Florida. I've never watched close-up while a house was being constructed on the beach before, but I've been amazed at how the building crews anchor these structures in the sand to withstand the coming years of erosion and weather.

In our case, at least, they took forty-four telephone poles—each thirty-five feet in length—and water blasted them deep into the ground at set locations. Then they connected all forty-four of those sunken phone poles with rebar, built a wooden frame around the whole apparatus, and poured enough concrete into that giant box to make a solid rock two feet thick, encompassing the whole footing area. Then they poured more concrete on top of that, reinforcing the foundation even further. Then they erected a whole network of rebar pillars—spaced about every three feet—stretching all the way up to the roof of the house. After that, they laid cinder blocks around each of those steel-enmeshed columns, and poured concrete down into them, tying the roof into the foundation.

That house isn't going anywhere until the Second Coming takes it.

I mention this because I know the Bible tells us to build our house "on the rock" instead of "on the sand" (Matt. 7:24–27). That's obviously some good, godly advice. But sometimes life—with all its third-and-long situations—doesn't give us much of anything else but sand to build on. And we've got to decide what kind of foundation we're going to plant there. Even in the sand. Whether we've done it to ourselves or had it forced on us by others, we don't have the option of blaming the surrounding landscape for the weaknesses in our personal character construction. Not if our intention is to build a winner—wherever we are.

You may not like the job you have right now, for example. You may not like *not* having a job right now. (I've certainly been there.) You may be having marriage problems. Difficulties with your children. Extreme stresses at work. Troubling health issues. Strained relationships. Mounting financial losses. Big worries.

You may feel like you're sinking in quicksand.

Scrambling to stay afloat.

But even here God knows what you need. More than you need rescue, more than you need your circumstances to correct themselves, you need what God often grows best in the sandy soil of these third-and-long struggles. You need the kind of nailed-down character priorities and promises He can water blast into your daily routine, anchoring your life on a foundation that's solid enough to stand strong, even in stormy conditions.

So do I.

So let's bring to Him whatever down-and-distance situations we're facing at the moment, commit them to His sovereign care and knowledge, and promise we'll quit trying to scramble our way out of these things, the way we've been doing. No more sending everybody long. No more tossing up prayers that aren't really meant to imply any lasting trust or commitment to Him. In trust and humility let's just focus on winning the battle at the line of scrimmage today. And the next day. And the next day. And all the other character days that are standing between us and an end zone of success and opportunity.

What follows in this book is my best stab at describing "winning character"—the kind that is sure to lead to success when we write it into our calendars each day with ink pen and don't change it for anything or anybody.

I've seen it. I hope I've lived it.

And I know we're not going anywhere without it.

PART I

Established Foundations

1

The Fine Line

They say there's a fine line between winning and losing. Let me tell you just how "fine" the "fine line" can be.

When the smoke cleared on the last week of the 2005 college football regular season—my seventh as head coach at Clemson—we missed claiming the ACC Atlantic Division title by one win.

Make that one *point*.

Following hard, back-to-back home losses to #17 Boston College (in overtime) and #13 Miami (in triple overtime), we had just begun clawing our way back into contention before dropping a late October game at Georgia Tech.

Final score, 10–9.

We had been inside their 10-yard line with less than six minutes to play, first and goal, trailing by four. Freshman wide receiver Aaron Kelly had run back the first kickoff return of his career 81 yards to give us the short field. But when Charlie Whitehurst's third-down pass was deflected at the line of scrimmage, incomplete, we decided to kick a chip-shot field goal to pull within one point.

Turned out to be a good call. Our defense held well enough to give us two more chances to score in the final minutes, one that died on a failed fourth-down attempt, less than ten yards out of reasonable field goal range, the other on a last-second interception. We were *that* close.

And even though we responded the next two weeks with blowout wins over Duke as well as my father's eventual ACC champion Florida State to close out the conference schedule, we could never overcome that one-point loss in Atlanta from mid-season. When it was all said and done, when the games were all played out, we were one point away.

Then came 2006—when we not only missed clinching our division again by one point, but by one *extra point*.

We had come into our week two rematch with Boston College ranked #18 in the country, and we established the lead early, going up 10–0 by the end of the first quarter, only to be caught from behind when they returned the second-half kick-off for a touchdown to tie the score at 17. Unfortunately that wasn't their only long kick return of the afternoon, including a thirty-yarder midway through the fourth period that gave quarterback Matt Ryan ample field position for a game-tying drive. (We certainly weren't the first—and probably won't be the last—to learn from *that* mistake with him.) Before we knew it, we were facing yet another overtime affair—our second straight against BC in two consecutive years.

The first overtime period ended with each of us trading field goals. 27–27. Then after getting the ball first to open the second overtime, we drove in for a go-ahead touchdown and were just about to turn the game over to our defense in hopes of finishing off a tough victory.

Only one problem. Our extra point was unexpectedly blocked.

I mean, how many times do you see that? Like, never? In overtime? Come on. But by giving our opponent such a late, sudden burst of momentum, it was no real surprise to see them close out their next scoring chance with a six-yard touchdown run, tying us momentarily at 33, followed by the deciding point-after to win the game.

And we ended up chasing that extra point all year long.

Five straight wins we reeled off next, including conference victories over Florida State (27–20), over North Carolina (52–7), over Wake Forest (27–17), and over Georgia Tech (31–7). Big wins. Strong performances. Our two tailbacks, James Davis and C. J. Spiller, combined to give us the top-scoring offense in all of college football.

But we stumbled hard at Virginia Tech on a Thursday night—again, the last week of October—losing 24–7. Then we dropped our second one-point heartbreaker of the season the following week, at home November 4 against Maryland, 13–12, a game we probably would've won if not for an illegal procedure penalty that nullified a late touchdown and left us settling for a field goal.

So, yeah, there's a fine line between winning and losing. There's an even finer line between winning games and winning championships. I should know. I won a lot of games in my twelve years as a head coach. Never had a losing season. Never failed to qualify for a bowl game. Even went undefeated one year in my second and final season at Tulane, 1998. Won our conference. Wound up seventh in the nation in the final polls—by far the highest ranking they'd achieved since their long-struggling football program had finished fifth overall way back in 1939. (That was the same year Riddell started experimenting with plastic helmets).

But I also know from tough, firsthand experience that you can be a really good team and still really lose. You can work hard all week and still fail to execute properly when the game is on the line. You can do a lot of things right and still be the one walking out of that stadium with your head down, crunching the ice underfoot on some other coach's Gatorade bath.

Sometimes all it takes is one little point.

One mistake.

One dropped ball.

One botched play. That's it.

And that doesn't just go for football either.

A good man can slip up in one area of his life and lose relationship with his wife and kids forever. A guy who's worked hard to build his business and advance his career can make one bad call, sign off on one questionable deal, agree to one unwise partnership, and watch everything disintegrate overnight—that is, if the fallout doesn't drag on slowly for months and years, draining him dry, not leaving him hardly any time to recover once it all falls apart.

It doesn't take much.

It's a fine line.

And that's why the daily, determined pursuit of character is so important to me—important enough for me to step out of my comfort zone here and risk putting a message down on paper like this, where everybody can read it and say anything about it (or about me) they want to.

I'm not a writer. I know that. But I'm a husband. And I'm a father. I'm a friend and a church member. I've got people I care about and a family worth fighting for. And, like you, I live in a world where the easy way is usually the most available way—and with few exceptions the most appealing way.

But I don't like losing any more than you do. Especially not by one point. And if there's anything I can say to help you and me realize just how diligent and resolved and immovable we must stay if we want to be successful in life—in all the most important ways—then I'm here to say it. And with God's help I'm here to live it.

And I assume you're here because you want the same thing.

The Fine Line Defined

I was a head coach for nearly twelve years at two major Division 1–A college football schools. For twenty years prior to that, I was an assistant coach at places like Alabama, Auburn, and Florida State. The pressure to win was enormous. The competition was intense. But as fierce as practice and game days can be when you're working in those kinds of high-octane arenas, nowhere does a coach feel quite as much ongoing stress as he does in recruiting.

And the NCAA doesn't help make that any easier.

The biggest thing they hate—the one dynamic they work the hardest to expunge from college athletics—is any activity that creates a recruiting advantage for one member institution over another. To this end (and because there's *no* end of creative minds in college coaching who never met a loophole they wouldn't like to exploit), the NCAA continues coming up with new ways to try keeping the playing field as fair as possible.

That's why they have *quiet* periods and *dead* periods— parts of the year when you're not allowed to watch practice, evaluate talent, or make face-to-face contact with a potential student athlete. That's why they limit the times when your official visits can occur, how many of these visits can be made, which of your personnel can recruit off campus, how and when and how often you can communicate with possible signees. Similar to the IRS, the rules can grow so ambiguous and hard to interpret sometimes, you're left to navigate a good bit of gray area. It may all sound right and reasonable on paper, but it's a tricky walk when you're actually out there on the recruiting trail, watching for land mines in real time.

One of the most awkward and uncomfortable situations to manage is when you're visiting a high school during certain times of the year—times when you're not allowed to talk to a player, when you're just there to see his football coach, to inquire about the young man's progress on the field and in class, to make enough of a splash to leave the impression that you're interested in this guy. You're hoping word gets back to him that you came out of your way to check on him, even though you couldn't tell him yourself. But perhaps at some point as you're walking into the gym on your way to the coach's office—*bam!*—there he is, right in front of you—the prospect you're not supposed to interact with.

What do you do?

Jump back from the door and hope he hasn't seen you? Dart your eyes around like you're just there to count the seating capacity in this place? The NCAA doesn't mind if you say something like, "Hey there, son, you understand I can't talk with you today. Sorry." But that's it. Comes under the heading "incidental contact," which they graciously admit is just flat-out impossible to avoid sometimes.

Put yourself in that position, however—a coach standing eyeball-to-eyeball with a choice ballplayer you'd love to have on your team, a guy you've been working like crazy to develop a trusted relationship with, a young man who's being wooed just as hard or harder by some of your top competition, and tell me you can't feel your jaw muscles working, the pressure building, how easy it would be to step outside and spend just a few minutes in one-on-one, chemistry-building conversation—a thousand miles from home, and a long, long way from NCAA headquarters.

But it's wrong. You know it.

And unless your moral compass is locked on true north, completely committed to living above every shortfall and suspicion, you will find yourself resorting to compromise—and figuring it's the best play you've got at the moment. The endless tug of winning, of needing to fill those eighty thousand seats in the stadium every Saturday, of attracting enthusiastic donations from deep-pocketed boosters to fund that $58 million athletic budget—it can feel well worth a little "secondary violation" or two, or three, or four.

Because it's such a fine line.

And every person in every generation must walk it . . . or risk taking a nasty spill on the other side of it.

The Fine Line at Work

Sitting here in 2012, I'm well aware that whatever's in the headlines this morning is likely much different from the stories you're reading today, no matter how many months or years in the future you happen to be standing from where I am right now. But this past college football season—2011—was marked as much by scandal as by on-the-field excitement— guys who tried nudging their way around that fine line and, in some cases, whose careers failed to survive when the fine line snapped back on them.

I think of Jim Tressel, now the former head coach at Ohio State University, a guy I've followed through the years and truly believe to be a solid, committed Christian man. Few people who've had any up-close dealings with him would disagree with that statement. I once spent some time with him and his wife, Ellen, on a weeklong trip. When I was at Clemson, his staff came down during an off season and visited with ours. Everything I've ever known or heard about Coach Tressel has always been top-drawer.

But based on what the NCAA's investigation revealed, he chose to look the other way after hearing that several of the key players from his 2010 team, including star quarterback Terrell Pryor, had received up to $14,000 in both cash and the value of discounted tattoos in exchange for signed jerseys and other Buckeyes memorabilia. When asked either to deny or verify the accuracy of these reports in September of that year—several months after he began trading e-mails to try shushing up the problem—he said he had no knowledge of any wrongdoing by any of these athletes. And when the proof finally did come into full light a few months later, right as the regular season was winding down, not only the head coach but the AD's office, the school administration, even the Big 10 Conference leadership permitted the offending students to go ahead and play in the Sugar Bowl against SEC opponent Arkansas.

Easy to predict they weren't going to win that ball game without those five crucial guys on the field. Playing *with* them, they did. But at what cost?

To tell you the truth, the kinds of dilemmas and decisions Coach Tressel faced in April 2010 are not at all uncommon in college athletics. Nearly every day in a head coach's life, some piece of paper comes across his desk. A bit of someone's conversation comes to his attention. An awareness of some potential trouble or misconduct comes up. And he's faced with a small handful of options for how to handle it. No doubt Coach Tressel had seen more than his fair share of these questionable scenarios over the years and had dealt with them in a brave, upright, truthful fashion. Most of the time. Maybe *all* of the time.

But for whatever reason, *this* time—to him—the issues that were involved seemed to be on the borderline. And once he'd crossed *that* line, his next decisions—the ones that got him into even deeper trouble and suspicion—became all too easy to justify.

In the end, with the scandal spinning out of control, he was left with no other option than to resign in May 2011 after a long, championship career, notwithstanding his self-imposed five-game suspension scheduled to begin the following season. Then in August it got even worse. The NCAA handed down a five-year "show-cause" penalty, effectively banning him from the college sidelines until 2016—most likely forever since he would be sixty-four years old by that time.

But that's what can happen—even to good men—when they don't slow down long enough to notice the fine line that exists between success and failure (like in Coach Tressel's case, having to work at the same school as my brother Terry now, who's the head coach at Akron University. I sure don't envy him that. Tressel has taken a fund-raising position there, the place where he began his coaching career as a graduate assistant.)

I think, too, of the situation with quarterback Stephen Garcia and Steve Spurrier, currently head coach at South

Carolina, against whom our Clemson teams waged several fierce rivalry battles during my tenure there. Midway through the 2011 season—finally—in the wake of five previous suspensions, Coach Spurrier kicked Garcia off the team after the fifth-year senior failed *another* alcohol test, one of the provisions of his zero-tolerance agreement with the university.

Throughout a tumultuous college career that eventually netted passing yardage totals and overall victories putting him in the top two or three highest-producing quarterbacks in school history, Garcia had run afoul of the law on numerous occasions. He had been arrested for drunkenness and failure to stop for a police officer. He had been charged with keying a professor's car in the school parking lot. And he had repeatedly placed himself in violation of team rules, most notably during the run-up to the 2010 Chick-fil-A Bowl in Atlanta. It was one thing after another.

Yet for all his misdoings, for all the spring practice and summer workouts that he was banned from participating in—and apparently for the perceived lack of playing ability to be found in all the other Gamecock quarterbacks who suited up during each of those five years—Garcia never missed a single game as a direct result of his bad behavior. Every shortcoming was met by a second, third, fourth, fifth, even sixth chance.

Here you can see a young, talented, but struggling athlete, making one poor decision after another, thinking he could sidestep the fine line without facing the consequences. You also see a coach trying to help and encourage him, motivated to keep him from destroying his reputation and his high potential for success. Yet Garcia continued to violate enough boundaries until Coach Spurrier was ultimately forced to do what he had to do. No other choice.

That fine line will get you every time.

And who can overlook the shocking events surrounding the Penn State football program and the sudden fall from grace of legendary coach Joe Paterno, whose sixty-two-year career with the school—forty-six as head coach—was cut off midyear by a sexual abuse scandal involving a former defensive coordinator.

Details of the Penn State situation are still seeping out at this current stage of the process, so forgive me if a lot of this is old news or has been interpreted a bit differently as you're reading this. The coach's death from lung cancer, of course, less than two months after his firing, made the whole ordeal even more tragic. Hard to imagine there wasn't some connection between the way his body responded to medical treatment and the way his heart was already grieving from what these revelations had cost him. But all indications to date point to at least secondhand knowledge by Coach Paterno of the types of offenses that had been committed in the locker-room showers. Allegedly, a certain member of the football staff had witnessed one such horrific event against a young boy and had notified the head coach, who apparently referred the matter to other officials within the athletic office, likely not wanting to confront an old friend with a charge that was as vile as it was unbelievable, knowing him as long as he had. We can only guess.

I'll be the first to admit, it's hard not to have a lot of respect for Joe Paterno and his unprecedented coaching legacy, parts of which I was privileged to witness up-close. My wife and I spent a full week each year with Coach Paterno and his wife, Sue, for ten straight years as part of vacation trips sponsored by Nike for their contract coaches. I also watched him and my father jockey back and forth, season after season, to find out who would amass the most victories in their long, storied careers. Their three-overtime slugfest in the 2006 Orange Bowl was a duel for the ages. And their race for coaching supremacy was less a battle and more a gentlemen's exercise in mutual esteem and admiration.

But no matter what the reasoning or rationale, the decision to avoid stepping into a messy, uneasy situation was wrong, no matter how distasteful it was or how badly he wished to avoid personal conflict. He admitted as much before he died.

And yet look what it cost him and his legacy. A man without peer in the annals of college coaching ended his career with something he'd *never* had for all those years, even as recently as a week or two before—a severely tarnished record to go along with his 409 career wins, two national championships, five undefeated seasons, thirty-seven bowl appearances, twenty-four bowl victories, twenty-three final finishes in the top ten national rankings—most of these all-time records among all the men who've ever coached the game.

And if it can happen to a guy like that, a man whose accomplishments placed him at the tip-top of a large heap, covering all the long, colorful decades of college football history, then who says it can't happen to somebody like you and me—ordinary fellows whose decisions today may not be the stuff of headline news but who still carry a lot of weight in our own homes and workplaces?

- It may be whether to click that enticing button that lets you scroll through a salacious new set of pornographic images on your Internet device.

- It may be whether to report a mistake you found that accidentally works to your favor in your expense reporting for the month.

- It may be whether to give a full tithe (or more) of your week's pay in the offering plate on Sunday.

- It may be whether to go to church at all, seeing as you were out late last night or you've got a lot of stuff to take care of around the house today—maybe a ball game to watch.

- It may be whether to walk away from a disagreement with your wife before you say something that could turn a one-night standoff into a weeklong, maybe monthlong, maybe *lifelong* battle neither one of you will ever forget.

It may be one of a million things. But each of them carries the potential of being that one-point difference standing between you and success in life. In order to win, in order to overcome, you're going to have to make real-time decisions based on trusted, age-old principles. You're going to have to tighten that moral compass until it doesn't budge one inch off-center for any other kind of magnetic pull. And you're going to have to do it every day.

Otherwise, even your close losses could turn into devastating defeats.

So Where Do I Start?

You'll find throughout the course of this book that I believe wholeheartedly in Jesus Christ. If I didn't, nothing I've written so far, and nothing you're about to read next, would be worth the paper it's printed on. We are so removed from being able to stay consistent and steady and poised and trustworthy over time, it's pretty ridiculous even to try. Attempting life without being in relationship with Christ is to expect one losing season after another . . . and to guarantee *complete* collapse in the end.

If you don't know what I'm talking about—if you're not sure what having a saving relationship with Jesus really means—I promise you this won't be the last time I bring it up. But for now let's put it this way: none of us has a prayer of pleasing God or living well unless He Himself does something to help us. We just don't have it inside. Character does not come standard on the base model when we're talking about human beings, no matter who we are or where we come from.

Thankfully, though, God *has* done something for us. He sent His Son to earth to live a perfect life and to die in our place on the cross, enduring the punishment we deserve so that He can extend to us the opportunity for our sins to be forgiven and our hearts completely changed from the inside out. By receiving Christ as Savior and following Him as Lord, everything necessary for you to succeed in life can be downloaded directly into your system.

All you have to do is believe.

"If you confess with your mouth, 'Jesus is Lord,' and believe in your heart that God raised Him from the dead, you will be saved" (Rom. 10:9). It's as easy to do as it is hard to comprehend. He paves the way, and we receive Him by faith. Done deal.

But that doesn't mean you're automatically immune from making mistakes or choosing unwisely as you go along. Being a Christian does not mean He completely takes over your steering mechanism, driving you wherever He wants you to go. Yes, He is sovereign. He can do whatever He wants. But

He has made it such that even those of us who've received God's grace by faith in Christ must surrender to His will again and again in the everyday matters of life. We must learn not to count on these stubborn, self-centered, self-righteous hearts of ours. We must dig deeper each day into the applied wisdom of His Word. And we must ask for His help in making the best decisions we can make, every time we're faced with another one.

Because even though our acceptance of Christ's death as payment for our sins assures us that we can live forever with Him, the game of life is still played down here at field level. And in the Sunday-to-Saturday rhythm that we know so well, life basically comes down to making decisions. Make more good decisions than bad—decisions based on the truths of the Bible—and you put yourself in much better position to experience His blessing and to be a blessing to others. Trust your own flighty judgment, however, even if you're a believer, hoping you're probably in the right frame of mind at most times of day or night to make the right choices? Well . . . good luck with that.

With a line this fine, you're just asking for trouble.

This life is no scrimmage. It's not spring ball. We're not wearing shorts and helmets, running half-speed through no-contact drills. This life—and this book—is a call to get serious, to realize we've only got a certain amount of time on earth to learn His ways, influence others, and put His gifts and investments to work in live action. Under the lights. On game day.

And since a new one starts tomorrow, I'm suggesting you join me right away in opening God's playbook to see what we're going to need for the challenges that are just around the corner.

It's a fine line we're walking. But walk it faithfully, courageously, without turning to the right or the left, and you can walk it straight into the best life God offers to mortal man.

2

The Power of Influence

Back in the days of Vince Lombardi and Hank Stram, about as close as most fans ever got to seeing a coach on the sidelines was through the carefully edited eye of NFL Films. Unless you were an active player or referee right down there on the field, or an assistant coach standing nearby, or one of the guys working the first-down chains directly in front of him, you were basically screened from seeing or hearing the head coach up-close during the game. Ticket holders in the stadium—even the ones with decent seats—could still only pick him out at a distance by the coat and hat he was wearing. True, they might be able to catch a *little* better look by zooming in on him through their binoculars, perhaps seeing his wild, flailing gestures at a badly missed tackle or a blown call by the officials. But in those days, a coach was able to act or react pretty much however he wanted without worrying that his voice or his likeness would ever be captured for public consumption.

Not anymore.

Today, I'm convinced, the television networks keep one camera trained exclusively on the head coach at all times during a broadcast, able to cut quickly to a close-up whenever he's likely to show disgust, outrage, or emotion in response to a game situation. Factor in those huge parabolic microphones they hold up on the sidelines to absorb and transmit live-action sound, and you're talking about a whole lot of opportunities for a coach's reflex reactions to become play-by-play material.

How many times have you heard the announcers say, "Well, you sure don't have to be a lip-reader to know what he thought about *that!*" It's all out there. Unvarnished. Uncensored.

Seems like I remember, in fact, when Bill Cowher resigned as head coach of the Pittsburgh Steelers in 2006, he mentioned that among his many reasons for stepping down was his own dismay at how angry and foul mouthed he appeared when he saw a tape of himself during game action. Didn't like the example he was setting for his children. (Maybe you wouldn't like it if your kids could watch *you* at work either.)

But here's the truth: *what we do affects others.* Things we don't even remember saying can still leave an impact years later. All day long we're making impressions, even when we don't realize we're being watched.

That's the power of influence. For good or bad.

And it's not only celebrities and publicly recognized figures who have to worry about it. Life in a post-9/11, ultra-technological society means cameras and cell phones are everywhere these days. We're rarely out from under public scrutiny and surveillance—any of us—at the store, on the street corner, at a traffic light. And even when we're safe inside our homes or offices, our wives and children and coworkers are usually there to pick up on everything else.

We're always influencing. Always.

So this matter of developing a "winning character" is not just a self-improvement exercise. The end result is not just to be a better person. One of the main reasons for wanting to work so hard to develop discipline and responsibility and any other good character trait is because people are counting on us. They're looking to see if our faith is all talk. They're curious to know how we're going to handle stressful situations. Sure, some people are only looking to be critical. We'll always have that. Many of them are trying to justify their own subpar behavior by pointing out little bits and pieces of hypocrisy in us. Makes them feel better about themselves if they can find fault in others.

But I think most of them, deep down, are wishing they could be better people inside. Don't all of us want that if we're being really honest? In watching us so closely and observing our lives—especially us Christians—I think they're actually looking for proof that something works. If they can truly see a difference in us, and if they can see it enough times with enough consistency, they might be convinced that, hey, "Maybe God really is my answer."

I know not many of us are all that great when it comes to making speeches or explaining things, especially when we're trying to put into words what life with Jesus Christ is all about and what He means. But maybe we wouldn't have to say as much if we'd just let our life do our talking for us.

Guess what? It already does.

Intentional Influence

As a head coach, I realized early on that putting a solid football team on the field wasn't my only job. Most of us who love sports and love coaching wouldn't mind a bit if the only thing we did, all day every day, was to tinker around with blocking styles and pass protections, with two-minute management and blitz packages. Put us anywhere near a chalkboard, and we're like kids in a sandbox. Can't get enough of it. We love the innovating, the cat-and-mouse game of outsmarting our opponents. Put a whistle around our necks on the practice field, and we want to stay there way past dark pushing our team to absolute perfection. We thrive on working for crisp execution, for flawless performance. When we go to bed at night, we're still thinking about it.

But as much as we love the game and the action—a lot more than some people probably realize we do—football isn't the only thing a coach teaches. He teaches life. He makes men. It may sound insincere to say, but that doesn't mean it's not true.

According to NCAA calculations, fewer than 2 percent of all college football players (1.7, to be exact) ever embark on a professional playing career. And some last for only a season or two. That leaves 98 percent or more of the average locker room anywhere in the country filled with young guys who'll spend the rest of their lives building houses, selling products, owning businesses, walking a police beat, stuff like that. They'll marry and raise a family (I hope) and take their place in ordinary, next-door-neighbor society. Football will always be a big part of their past, of course, but probably a much smaller part of their future.

So as a coach, I knew I owed each player on my team a lot more than just the good ole college memory of beating an in-state rival or the experience of going to a bowl game. I owed him something he'd need later on, like maybe on one of those cold, rainy, miserable mornings when getting up to go to work was the last thing he felt like doing. I owed him something his future wife and children could look up to. I owed him something that could help him become as strong a man on the inside at fifty as he was on the outside at a young, muscular twenty.

I owed him my influence.

And I worked hard to give it to him. To all of them.

For starters, I made sure I was in church on Sunday. And I made sure my team understood how much importance I placed on that—not just for me but for them too.

Going back to my days as an assistant coach, I must have relocated my family twelve or thirteen times. Kinda lost count, to tell you the truth. All I remember for sure is that we moved a whole bunch. But in every new town we lived in, one of the first things my wife and I did—right off the bat—was to get involved in a local church. First thing.

During football season that often meant getting up at 5:30 in the morning, driving into the office to grade my film, then rushing back home to pick up Linda and the children so we could make it in time for Sunday school and church. As a head coach, it got even harder, especially when they started wanting to tape my television show on Sunday mornings at 6:00. But that just meant setting the alarm a little earlier—4:00, 4:30—to get prepped and ready for the studio, then back home, then back out. I'd already put in a good day's work by the time I sat down for worship.

But church mattered. Not in some manipulative way. Not to score brownie points with God or to check off my "do-gooder" box for the day. Being an active, engaged member of a local church was important to me on a lot of levels—obedience to God's Word, the spiritual health of my family, ongoing account- ability with other Christians, my own need for good Bible teach- ing, my debt of worship to God for His grace and salvation and forgiveness of my sins. But it was even more than that. I under- stood, too, that my players needed somebody in their lives who was constantly encouraging them to stay close to the Lord. Not just with talk but with actions.

If I didn't do it, who would? Anybody?

Maybe. But maybe not.

A lot of these young men had spent the first seventeen, eighteen years of their lives in church. They may not have had a saving faith in Jesus Christ to show for it, but their bodies had at least been in the building at worship time. Mama and Daddy had made sure of that. So I hated to think of some of these boys being on campus the next four or five years, away from home and family, getting totally out of the habit of church attendance, slipping further and further away from God. I wanted to give them at least one person in authority who was pointing them in the right direction, every chance I got.

And I really did. One of the last things we talked about in the locker room on Saturday—after going over the highs and lows of the game, after making announcements about the next practice, after discussing their treatment schedules and so forth—was to tell them that I hoped they'd be in church tomorrow. They sure knew *I'd* be going. And in a town as small as Clemson, South Carolina (population twelve thousand, not counting the students), people in the community noticed when their football players were up and dressed for worship on Sunday. Whether these guys knew it or not, *they* carried a lot of influence too.

So on Saturdays after a game, I reminded them that God was the One who had blessed them with the ability to play football, that He had given them this opportunity for a reason. And I told them that one of the best, most immediate ways they could show Him their thanks was by going to His house in the morning and telling Him so.

That's influence. And everybody's got it.

You too.

Ordinary Influence

You may be one of those people who don't think you've got a lot to say, that you don't have much of an impact on others. You hear me talking about leading a group of eighty-some-odd ball players, directing a staff of assistant coaches and other personnel, and you don't see where you've got anybody like that in your life who really cares enough to listen to you. You're too invisible, you think. Too ordinary.

Let me remind you that when Jesus Christ came to Earth more than two thousand years ago, God chose to confine

His Son's active, public ministry to about three years total. And for the first part of that time—perhaps as much as a full year—Jesus went out looking for some men to help Him, to be part of what He was initiating. He didn't have much time to get this done, and He needed some real difference-makers. Military men? Roman officials? Religious scholars? That's who you'd think He'd be looking for. For a job this big, only the best would do, right? All-stars. Dream team.

And yet of the twelve men Jesus selected to be His closest disciples, as many as five to seven of them were fishermen. Blue collar. Working class. Another was a tax collector. One was a zealot (something like a tea party activist). Every one of them were just ordinary men, pulled off the fishing boat, pulled away from their desk and their daily obligations.

But by the time Jesus got through influencing them and filling them with His Spirit, the Bible says they had "turned the world upside down" (Acts 17:6). In fact, we're still sitting here talking about them today, all these many years later. Little kids in church sing songs with the names of these men set to music. Every morning when we open our Bibles, there they are! Still teaching us. Still encouraging us. Still telling us about what Jesus did, what they learned from Him, what He was able to accomplish through their oh-so-ordinary lives.

Everybody—I mean *everybody*—has influence.

I've got five brothers and sisters. Two of them have law degrees. One has his master's, another his doctorate. Me? I've got a padded folder around here somewhere with my diploma from West Virginia University, a physical education degree, inscribed with the school president's signature but (thankfully) not my grade point average, which was C-range at best.

But you know what? God has used me just like He uses anybody else—just like He's using *you*, right where you are, to make a difference in people's lives, especially as His character takes deeper and deeper root in your life.

For me, having an influence might be mentioning to a few players standing around me at afternoon practice to look up at that purple sunset in the western sky and tell me there's not a Creator God in heaven. For you it may be talking to your kids about the wonders of nature while you're out working in the yard or grilling hamburgers on the back deck.

For me, having an influence might be praying over my team at the close of spring ball before they take off for Florida or who-knows-where for spring break, asking God to keep them safe and bring them back in one piece. For you, it may be stopping to ask a blessing when you sit down to eat lunch at work, or keeping a Bible out visible on your desk, or starting a weekly prayer time with a few like-minded friends at the break table.

For me, having an influence might be never letting myself stoop to using foul language, even when there was *no way* that guy's foot was in bounds when he caught that pass, even when one of my players' stupid penalties cost us getting the ball back at a crucial moment of the game. For you, it may just be choosing not to make an off-color comment, or to laugh at somebody else's, even when a really funny one pops into your mind.

But it's all influence. And it's all critically important.

The Bible says that not even a sparrow can fall to the ground without God the Father knowing about it. Even the "hairs of your head," Jesus said, "have all been counted" (Matt. 10:29–30). People say, "Oh, I don't matter that much. I don't think God even knows I'm here." But that's not what His Word says. "Look, I have inscribed you on the palms of My hands; your walls are continually before Me" (Isa. 49:16). He knows where you live. He knows what's happening with you. He knows all the things He can enable you to be.

Because whether you like to think of yourself as having influence or not . . . *you do*. If you're a parent, you have influence. If you've got friends you hang around with, you have influence. If you go to school or go to work, you have influence. If you manage a business or teach a classroom full of students, you have influence.

The question is not whether you've got it. The question is what kind of influence it's going to be.

And the answer lies in your character.

Influence in Action

Second commandment. Exodus 20. That's where the Bible talks about not making idols for ourselves, not bowing down and worshipping anything other than God alone. It's one of those "thou shalt nots" of Scripture. And as far as this one goes, most of us don't think we do. *Idols? Us?*

- But when we get in the habit of wasting time and being lazy, we make an idol of whatever we find so fascinating—the television, the Internet, the movie theater, whatever.

- When we don't give other people permission to be honest with us, when we're unwilling to examine our heart to see if whatever they're saying about us might be true, we make an idol of our own independence and arrogance.

- When we downplay or ignore the needs of our family, while at the same time saying yes to anything else our job, our friends, or others ask of us—no matter how unreasonable—we make an idol of our public reputation.

- When we excuse our behavior as just being part of our nature, or when we blame other people for forcing us to feel or act a certain way, we make an idol of our favorite, most comfortable sins.

- When we buy things we don't need yet feel cold and offended by people who ask for things *they* seem to need, we make an idol of our money, our stuff, our position in life.

As the sixteenth-century Christian reformer John Calvin said, our heart is a "factory of idols." We build them up as fast as we can dream them. We hoard them. We love them. We worship them. And God, in His willingness to let us make our own decisions, gives us the freedom to craft as many of these idols as we want.

But according to that passage in Exodus 20, one freedom automatically goes out the window when we design idols for ourselves, when we sacrifice character on the altar of our selfishness. *We lose the freedom to keep those idols to ourselves.* When we start making compromises, living for other things and other reasons than for God alone, our idols don't just end up influencing *us.* They influence others.

"You must not bow down to them or worship them," God warns us, "for I, the LORD your God, am a jealous God, punishing the children for the fathers' sin, to the third and fourth generation of those who hate Me" (Exod. 20:5). The child whose father won't control his temper, won't discipline himself, won't resist his sinful appetites—that son or daughter will be impacted in some way by those so-called "personal" decisions that his or her parent makes. God's Word says so, and our experience bears it out.

Divorced couples tend to come from divorced families. Abusive dads tend to grow abusive kids. Dysfunction begets dysfunction. Our lack of character will often show up in our own children and in the particular struggles they face throughout life.

Influence. It's a hard, biblical concept.

But thank God, it doesn't have to be so pessimistic. The same grace that works in us, empowering us to overcome temptation, to develop good habits, to grow solid character, to trust God's wisdom more than our own opinions, comes with another influential promise that's at least twenty-five times better than its ugly cousin. That same "jealous" God who wants our undisputed devotion—the One who holds us accountable by warning us about the effects of our own decisions on our children—also promises to show "faithful love to a *thousand* generations of those who love Me and keep My commands" (Exod. 20:6).

Obviously, God is a lot more interested in helping us make our influence a positive one than a negative one.

The only thing He *won't* do is allow it to be a nonexistent one.

You are right now influencing your spouse, your children, your friends, your neighbors, your employees, your coworkers, your grandkids, everybody who knows you well at all. Doesn't matter if you mean to be. You just are.

But again, what kind of influence are you having? Is it good or bad? Is it helpful or harmful? Is it compelling people to faithfulness or leading them into trouble?

Those are the questions you and I need to live with.

The Main Ingredient of Influence

Do you want to be a person of significant influence? Do you want to make a difference in people's lives? Would you love to hear somebody say, "I'll never forget something you told me one time," or, "You're a guy I've always known I could count on, somebody I've always looked up to"?

You don't become that guy just by being smart or well read, by having a certain professional position, by being otherwise rich and successful. You become that guy by having a solid, consistent ethic that God can call on at any time—unannounced, at a moment's notice—in the ordinary flow of an average day or the easy banter of a routine conversation.

Influence comes from character.

That statement reminds me of somebody who's had a tremendous influence on my life and career, not only because he was an authority figure over me for several important years, but because he is truly a guy whose walk matches his talk. I've seen it up close, in pressure situations. He's earned the right for his opinions to matter to me. And they do. They always have. They always will.

I was on Steve Sloan's staff at Duke University in the mid-1980s, a young assistant coach to a guy who had a real mind for the offensive side of the ball. A great play caller. Sharp football instincts. Coach Sloan had risen to prominence as a star quarterback at the University of Alabama in the early '60s, playing alongside (and often in front of) Joe Namath on some of Bear Bryant's most successful teams, winning two national championships as a player. He went on to a brief run in the NFL with the Atlanta Falcons, then began his college coaching career with two stints as offensive coordinator, one at Florida State and the other at Georgia Tech. Some of his most notable success came at Vanderbilt, his first head coaching job, where he propelled that beleaguered football program to only its second bowl game in school history in 1974. That's a long drought. No small accomplishment.

Several years later, from 1983 to 1986, he took a chance on me and gave me the opportunity to hone my leadership skills on the college sideline, first as wide receivers coach, then as offensive coordinator for his Duke Blue Devil teams. Working for such a committed man was an honor. He was committed not only to football and winning but also to his family and to Christ. What a godly man he was . . . and is!

On many, many occasions, long after the time we spent together there in Durham, I've continued to go to him for counsel and advice whenever I've needed a friend to talk to. In fact, if I had a big decision to make this afternoon, he would still be one of the first people I'd call to find out what he thought I should do. When he tells me he'll be praying for me, that's no canned Christian promise. He means it. And I count on it.

The one thing that leaps to mind, though, when I think of Coach Sloan is a piece of advice he gave me as a young husband and father. More importantly, it was a piece of advice I saw him heeding himself by his own personal example. I don't know what the divorce statistics are for men in the coaching profession. I'm sure they're high. The extreme demands at that level of football translate into a lot of time separated from your wife and family. It's tough. A lot of those marriages don't make it—not when you're married to football.

But he mentioned to me one time, as we were talking about how easy it is as coaches to put our families on the back burner, that he always tried to spend a portion of each Friday during the football season with his wife. Whatever else anybody wanted from him for those few hours on Friday afternoon, they all took a backseat to that one special, scheduled appointment of his.

That statement stuck with me.

Based on that one single conversation, I made a point during my twelve years as head coach, both at Tulane and at Clemson, to have lunch with my wife every Friday. I know in some ways that doesn't sound like much. But believe me, when you're working (by necessity) 95, 100, 110 hours a week, the easiest person in the world to put off till later is the girl you married. An hour or two at home, at your kitchen table, at a nearby restaurant, or even at your messy desk with a fast-food hamburger, means you've had to reshuffle your schedule pretty hard to do it. But through one man's influence—through a simple, unrehearsed statement on an otherwise ordinary day—my life was blessed enormously.

That's power. The power of influence.

And that's what every one of us wants to have. And *can* have. When we focus on letting God grow His character in us, influence will simply trail along as a by-product. It's not something you go out and seek. It's something that comes bundled up with the whole integrity package, and it finds its way out when you're not even noticing.

You are a person of influence. Use it wisely.

3

Growing Up Bowden

Trust me, it wasn't easy to get through a whole chapter on "influence" without mentioning even *once* the person who's impacted my life and career more than anybody else. But there's a good reason for that oversight. I always thought if I was ever to write a book about myself and my beliefs, my father would merit a chapter all to himself because I wouldn't be anywhere near the person I am today if not for him (as well as for my mother, Ann, of course). The two of them model what *influence* and *character* look like.

Not just in public. Not just on television.

At home. Where it counts.

When I was growing up, my dad hadn't yet become the household name he is today—five-time national coach of the year at Florida State, finishing fourteen straight seasons in the top five, winner of numerous New Year's Day bowl games, holder of many all-time college coaching records. Two different organizations now award annual trophies bearing his name, one to an outstanding coach who exemplifies character and integrity, one to the college player each year who most notably excels on the field, at school, and in the community.

Everybody knows Bobby Bowden.

Everybody.

But during my junior high years, "everybody" in Morgantown, West Virginia, could've opened up their white pages at the kitchen counter and found out the Bowdens' home address, could've seen what our phone number was. There was nothing all that glamorous in those days about being an assistant coach at the local university. Nobody camped outside our house or clamored hard for an interview. My father had a job. Everybody else's father had a job. Just wasn't that big of a deal.

My dad was actually my Sunday school teacher.

Things did change a bit, however, around the time I entered my senior year of high school, when successful West Virginia head coach Jim Carlen resigned to become coach at Texas Tech University and Dad was promoted from offensive coordinator to take Carlen's place. Granted, this was pre-ESPN, pre-twenty-four-hour sports talk. There was only one local newspaper in town. There were no Internet recruiting services for alumni to scan with their morning coffee, anywhere in the country, critiquing the current signing class. But still, it was a notable position on the big-time football stage. Suddenly we weren't quite so invisible. The pressure to perform in public view at a high level was about to become a noticeable reality for my father, even though his internal drive had always been there and had always been the same.

And if anybody was going to see whether this new job was going to change him, it would be the people who poured their milk from the same jug as he did every morning.

Some things never change.

Safe at Home

When I look around at the biggest challenges affecting men today, areas where they're not stepping up to the plate, the first one that comes to mind for me is the home. I'll be touching on this subject a lot more later on, but too many men today—too many husbands and fathers—are not owning up to their family responsibilities. They're busy at work, and they're read up on the kinds of things they like to talk about with their friends, but they're letting other people be the chief influencers in their children's lives. They're not staying intentional about showing them, through their own consistent example, what it means to follow God, to practice what they preach, and to handle adversity with a steady faith and trust in the Lord.

Let me tell you, my dad did.

One of the first things I noticed about him, just observing through teenage eyes, was that he didn't bring his work home with him. I'm sure there were plenty of days when his team wasn't performing the way he'd like, when his blood pressure was up, when the nonstop demands of coaching had worn down his patience. But I can sit right here and say, I never once saw him come in the door angry. (Of course, when he came home, he quickly found out who the *real* head coach was—my mother!) Still, I never saw him fly off the handle, kick the dog, start ordering us around. He didn't transmit his irritations to us, blowing off steam and then huffing away mad. Just always seemed to have that calm, unruffled demeanor. He didn't make us share the weight of his outside frustrations.

But even though I remember noticing this about my father, even as a kid, I didn't really learn to appreciate it until I became a head coach myself.

Every morning when the day starts, a college coach never knows what's going to crop up between now and nighttime. You've got eighty-five teenagers to account for. One might get caught cheating on a test. One might stop in to tell you his parents are getting a divorce. One might've just found out he'd gotten his girlfriend pregnant. Every day it's something else. You just wait for the next shoe to drop.

And that's not even the football part. The media part. The meetings part. The support staff and personnel part. There are conference calls to make, injuries to monitor, sloppy drills and bad attitudes to correct. Questions, concerns, trouble, disagreements.

You just don't feel like whistling into the driveway at night, dying to know how everybody's day went. Not usually.

I'm sure you know exactly what I'm talking about. I imagine most of *your* days don't usually wrap up either without experiencing a few headaches, dilemmas, and unlikable people along the way. The whole thing can send you home cross and edgy, with your fuse burned down pretty low. Doesn't take much at that point to set it off.

But I learned from watching my father how much grief and drama a man can spare his family when he parks his daily troubles at the back door. It helps keep his home settled, keeps everybody loose and able to be themselves. It's a gift you can bring home with you every afternoon or evening, and it doesn't cost you a thing—just a deep breath and a promise to save it for tomorrow, for somebody else who can actually do something about it.

That character lesson from my father means a lot to me.

Advanced Adversity Training

Here's another one. I hear coaches talk about how they don't read the papers, don't listen to the radio, don't pay any attention to what people are saying about them and their football program.

I also know a lot of them are lying.

Plenty of coaches keep a weather eye out when it comes to gauging public perception, always checking to see which way the wind's blowing. Afraid of their bad press, they let all the crying and the criticism get under their skin, making them question what they're doing, forcing them to bend to the pressure—who to play, how much to throw the ball, whether to make a scholarship offer to a local kid who's good for headlines but maybe not a good fit for the team.

But I know when I was coaching, I honestly didn't listen to any of that stuff. At all. I'm not saying I was *naïve,* of course. I could sure feel it when the fans were unhappy with me, with the team, with my choice of quarterbacks and such. Good people like Tim Bourret, my sports information director at Clemson, kept me abreast of the mood in the media, mainly so I wouldn't get caught blindsided at a press conference and look like I'd been in a cave for six months (which I basically *was* during football season, buried under the weekly pressures of recruiting and game preparation).

I don't think I'd have been ready to handle the onslaught, however, if I hadn't seen my father brace up under criticism when he'd dealt with it as a head coach himself. He was just incredible in adversity. Seemingly oblivious to it. Never even acted like he acknowledged it. Just went about his business, confident that he was doing the right thing—and more importantly, sure that God would fight his battles for him if he kept himself humble and principled.

Fortunately, my dad didn't endure but just a couple of losing seasons at the helm, which kept him from inviting the kind of criticism that follows a lot of coaches around. But I can sure remember the 1974 season at West Virginia, a team I played on as wide receiver, when he struggled to a 4–7 finish and drew some of the ugliest outbursts of fair-weather fandom I'd ever witnessed firsthand. It was just terrible—in the newspapers, on campus, everywhere you went. A lot of folks wanted to see him fired. I remember people standing up behind me at basketball games, not realizing I was his son, and just cursing him out when he'd walk by. That may not have been as bad as the death threats he received following his 1970 game with Pitt—the annual "Backyard Brawl"—where West Virginia blew a twenty-seven-point halftime lead to lose 36–35. But that particular backlash was quick, immediate, on to the next game. This other one, though, was incessant, withering, brutal.

I'm sure you've seen the kind.

And yet you'd see my father at home, and it was like nothing was happening. He just handled it. He was able to pocket that pressure somewhere else.

And you know how I think he did it?

Routinely, when we'd come down to breakfast in the morning—for as far back as I can remember—my father would already be sitting at the table, reading and studying his Bible. He still does it to this day. Oh, I'm not sure he gets up as early now as he used to . . . unless he's got an early tee time! But I know if I had happened to be in their home today, this very morning, it wouldn't have been uncommon for me to see him down there at the kitchen table, spending time with the Lord at the start of the day. He would sure have been off doing it somewhere in the house.

As a head coach let me tell you . . . that was a lot better place to be at 6:30 each morning than in the newspapers or on the computer. And the same thing goes for real estate brokers, bank executives, factory workers, young professionals just breaking in. Whatever you do, wherever you are, there's still no substitute for beginning each day in the Word. God still speaks to His people through the Scripture. It is "living and effective and sharper than any double-edged sword, penetrating as far as the separation of soul, spirit, joints and marrow. It is able to judge the ideas and thoughts of the heart" (Heb. 4:12).

The Bible keeps truth separated out from the noise. Keeps life in perspective. Keeps you focused on the main thing. Keeps other people's criticisms contained inside your greater priorities—God's priorities, eternal priorities. For a Christian the Bible is the way to hear your Savior reminding you, over and over, "I have told you these things so that in Me you may have peace. You will have suffering in this world. Be coura-- geous! I have conquered the world" (John 16:33).

That's another character lesson from my father that means a lot to me.

Habit Forming

I'll share just one more. I mentioned in the last chapter how important I considered church involvement to be and how I worked hard to model and motivate that principle in my players. But this wasn't just a conviction I developed as an adult. It wasn't an attempt to overcompensate for some glaring lack or flaw in my upbringing. My devotion to the church and my commitment to being an active part of its ministry started early in my life.

At home.

When I was coming along, I don't care if there was three feet of snow on the ground and a sidewalk to shovel, *we were going* to church. We were going to Sunday school. We were even going back that night for worship service and Training Union. (If you grew up Baptist, back at the time when I did, you know Training Union is what separated the Sunday morning crowd from the true, dedicated believers!)

And while, yes, there can be a lot of habit, routine, and legalism wrapped up in going to church every week, there's also something about setting a standard for your kids—a standard that may be unpopular at the time but one that trains them to know what's good for them while their hearts and beliefs are being formed.

I see a lot of men today, when their kids get to be about fourteen, fifteen, sixteen years old, letting them sort of set their own schedules, determine what they're going to do, live like little grown-ups, enjoying all the freedom of adulthood with little of the accompanying responsibility. When children who are turned loose like that say they don't want to go to church anymore, their parents don't usually feel like they can make them.

Well, that is not the way I was raised. Nor is it the way I raised my own family. There are some things your kids just don't get a vote on, in my opinion. And among them is whether they can determine for themselves if they're going to be an active part of your church.

The writer of the Bible book of Hebrews warns us about "staying away from our meetings, as some habitually do" (10:25). He understood how deeply we need the encouragement we derive from being with our church family. We need to worship, to be reminded of God's promises and warnings. We need to be with other believers. And so do our children.

To me, the church is just too important of an influence on their spiritual lives and the direction God wants to take them to have it removed so casually from their field of vision. Kids today hear a lot of voices speaking into their head—from friends, pop culture, general expectations—not to mention the loud, hungry voice that comes from their own sinful flesh and self-will. And you know as well as I do, a large percentage of the influences they hear from outside and feel from within are telling them lies they don't need to believe.

No, the church is not perfect. Not by a long shot. Nor is it the answer for everything. Nobody can stand on his church membership alone and hope it's enough to save him, not without receiving Jesus Christ as personal Lord and Savior. But we owe our children regular exposure to the church, as well as the steadfast example of our own personal commitment to its purposes, its people, its leaders, its ministries—most importantly, to its Bridegroom.

That's what my father did for me. He was committed to his faith, and, boy, he would not let himself deviate from that, not one bit.

But really, it just went along with his whole commitment to character and integrity. As committed as he was to Christ, to his family, to his church, and to the Word of God, he was equally committed to living with honor and honesty in his chosen profession—which, let me tell you, is a tough job. I guess all jobs are, really, but the pressure cooker of major college football is an animal all its own. It'll eat your character alive the second you turn your back on it.

I was fortunate, though, to be able to enter the coaching ranks having seen in my father not only a *successful* but also a *sterling* example and role model.

Too many young men get their start on coaching staffs where the head guy doesn't exactly play by the rules. He uses his social skills to skirt around the edges and hope everybody is impressed enough by him not to notice (or want to notice) what he's doing. His recruiting habits are less than straightforward, and the assistants who watch him at up-close range assume that's just how things are done.

But I was blessed to get the best of both worlds—not only a father who cared about being a godly authority figure within the windows and walls of his own home but also a man I was able to follow into his same line of work, observing in person how Christian character could be specifically applied to the day-to-day experience of college coaching.

That's a debt I'll never be able to repay.

The gift of character.

Still the One

Not too long ago my wife and I were in Atlanta and took the opportunity to stop by and visit my son, where he and *his* wife are currently working and living. As hard as it can be sometimes to get your kids ready for life and launched out on their own, and as strange as it feels to grow accustomed to their not being little and under your roof anymore, it is so rewarding to see them out there beginning their own adventure. Makes it all worthwhile.

We got to meet my son's boss for dinner one night, along with Ryan and his wife. And during the course of our meal together, he was kind enough to share the sort of compliments every parent loves to hear about his child—how hard our son was working, how well he was performing, what a pleasure it was to have him on the team. What else would you expect in a set-up situation like that?

What I *didn't* expect, however, was the moment when he came to a pause after one of those nice statements of his, and in the brief opening before I could say, "Thank you," my son turned toward me at the table, looked me in the eye, and said, "Dad, I just didn't want to disappoint you."

Yeah. I know that feeling well.

My dad, of course, would be the first to tell you he's made plenty of mistakes and doesn't want people thinking he's any more special than anybody else. Like with all of us, there's a lot of truth to that statement. But as his son—who became one of his ball players, who spent time as one of his assistants, who later even stood on the opposite sideline as a competing coach—I've gotten to see my father from just about every vantage point a man can be observed. And I can assure you, the Bobby Bowden everybody knows is the same Bobby Bowden I know.

And that kind of influence leaves a guy like me feeling one strong conviction: *I would never want to disappoint him.*

I sure hope I haven't.

My father worked hard. He prayed hard. He dreamed big and married well. He put good people around him everywhere he went. And God proved true to His Word by blessing him with everything required to be a solid influence for the gospel. I'm proud to be his son.

But I guess what I'm even prouder of is that today, on the other side of active coaching, he's still as motivated as ever to keep exercising that same influence, traveling to places most weeks of the year to speak before eager crowds about his faith in Christ. He doesn't get to fly in those private, chartered planes anymore—the ones available to him at short notice as head coach at Florida State. Instead he flies commercial now as a rule, finding the old southern adage to be all too true: even to get to heaven, you have to go through Atlanta.

But the kind of momentum that keeps him on the go, inspiring audiences across the country with his faith-based speaking, tells me Dad's identity was never so much "football coach" as "follower of Christ"—the One he trusted at an early age and never, ever quit on. When my father put his "hand to the plow," like Jesus talks about in Luke 9:62, he drove a straight row the whole way and hasn't stopped driving ever since. Even in his eighties, he is still living for what mattered most to him as a young believer, a husband, and a father with six kids at home.

Like I said, some things never change.

Like Bobby Bowden.

PART II

Character Building

4

House of C-A-R-D-S

There's no such thing as working your way in slowly as a college football coach. You're not given a ramp-up period where you get to know everybody, take a leisurely lunch or two with your new coworkers, learn your way around the facility, find out where they keep the copier and the coffeepot. From the second your feet hit the ground—like mine did on a warm Wednesday afternoon in New Orleans, December 11, 1996—it is full systems go.

And that's exactly the way I wanted it.

I had been an assistant coach for nineteen years leading up to that point. I'd watched other guys like me get their call up the ladder, heading off in pursuit of their coaching dreams. I'd followed their trajectories from a distance, imagining how I'd handle the same situation if I was in their shoes. And I was confident, given the opportunity, that I could be successful running my own program. I just knew it.

So after hearing about the head coaching position coming open at Tulane University, then being contacted by their athletic director to gauge my initial interest, I was eager to keep the conversation going. It started with a three-hour interview, conveniently scheduled at a small West Georgia airport a short drive from Auburn, Alabama, where I was currently on staff. After that I was invited the following weekend to an on-campus visit with the school president, several board members, as well as a small panel of current players. Before I left town, they had offered me the job.

Yes—I understood Tulane hadn't posted a winning record in more than fifteen years. I was fully aware that it was a private school where even the running backs had to be able to write a three-point paper and solve their own trig problems. I wasn't under any delusions about the challenge that awaited me.

But I also knew this: only about 115 schools in the country were playing Division 1-A college football at that time, and I was about to join the small, privileged fraternity of men who coached them. I truly believed I was ready.

I'd *better* be . . . because as fast as things had developed over the past few weeks to put me into this new position, they were about to start moving even faster.

Fresh from my introductory 4:00 p.m. press conference, I went directly into a team meeting with my new players. That's when I could feel my excitement really building. These were *my* guys, *my* team; and even though it was still the middle of December, I was already itching for the chance to take the field with them. Couldn't wait to see them out there, executing my system, watching it come to life on Saturday afternoons next fall under the lights at the Superdome.

But as much as I wanted to sit down right then with each one of them, get to know them individually, start making an immediate personal connection, I knew it'd probably be weeks before I'd see *any* of them again, even though we'd only met for the first time. Because when a head coach takes over, the immediate focus is on *recruiting*. And nothing—not even building relationship with your current team—takes precedence over that.

It leads to a lot of questions. And fast answers.

Quick:

- Which prospects have already made commitments with the former coaching staff?
- Is the AD going to force us to honor those, even the players who don't fit our new system?
- How many scholarships are still available to hand out?
- How many seniors are we losing?

- How many offensive linemen, defensive backs, receivers, starters?

All of this analysis goes up on what you call your "recruiting board," a comprehensive collection of player data, contact information, and game film, covering dozens of high school athletes that are on your program's radar. It's crucial that you find out who you've got, what you need, and where you intend to go looking for it.

Then meanwhile, almost simultaneously (as if this recruiting stuff weren't enough all by itself to consume every blink of your attention), you're busy assembling your new staff . . . and dismantling the old one.

Incoming head coaches handle this task in a variety of different ways. Some go right ahead and issue a general pink slip for everybody who's left over from the former regime. But, you know, that just didn't sit right with me. That's not the way I'd want to be treated myself under similar circumstances. So even though I came into the job with two full pages of possible candidates and coordinators that I'd been adding to my wish list over the years, I felt like, from a professional standpoint, I owed every current coach the chance to meet with me face-to-face. I knew I wasn't likely to keep many of them, probably not more than one or two. But I at least wanted to hear them out and discover what they brought to the table. And if I opted to go another direction—which I did, in most cases—at least I wouldn't just say it with a piece of paper. I'd say it with a handshake.

So starting at 8:00 the next morning—one after another in rolling, twenty-minute slots—I interviewed each and every member of the existing coaching staff. Then later in the day, as soon as the last one had left my office, the few of us who remained held our first coach's meeting, on what else—*recruiting*—working way into the night, just like we'd work every day and night from then on, as far as the eye could see.

That's the way it goes. Right from the start. Full bore. Full time.

It's crazy. There's no other word for it.

But as crazy as the life of a college football coach can be, it's not as crazy as thinking you can excel at something so impossibly complex just by working hard and hoping for the best. There's always more to any undertaking than getting good at the particular skills that relate most directly to the task at hand.

The same goes for you too—in your *own* impossibly complex situations.

Life is life, whether it's football life, family life, business life, church life, community life, whatever. And the keys to making it all come together into something that resembles success are the same across the board.

The difference is character. *Winning* character.

That's why, even as I was circling every possible wagon on the recruiting trail as a new head coach, even while I was working the phones constantly to put together a top-notch staff, I was also churning on some core principles I'd been storing in my arsenal over the years, waiting for the right time to fold them into my coaching style.

I was pretty confident that I could map out a solid offensive and defensive philosophy, a philosophy for special teams, a philosophy for practice, a philosophy for academics. But I knew if I didn't bundle it all together into a shared commitment to *character*, my team would find itself all too often on the wrong side of that fine line between winning and losing. And I certainly didn't want to waste the kind of effort this job would require on something that wasn't going to pay off in every way.

No, I didn't have it all figured out exactly. I hadn't even coached a single game yet. But I was already beginning to narrow down my overarching game plan to five key basics that I believed would form the foundation of a winning program, no matter how effective our passing attack was or who was throwing the ball.

I truly believe these five things will prove to be difference-makers for you too. With God's help they can lead you toward being successful at anything you want to do.

The Winning Hand

Here they are. I'll go ahead and give them to you.

Commitment.

Accountability.

Responsibility.

Discipline.

Sacrifice.

Five strong, concrete words and concepts.

I'd imagine, though, just seeing them stacked up in a row like this, one on top of the other, that they don't surprise you or strike you as being anything out of the ordinary. Not a one of these ideas is remotely foreign or unfamiliar to you—or even unexpected. You could read right past them without breaking stride and find yourself several paragraphs down before you looked up, still not recognizing what you'd missed.

But isn't that the way true strength most often shows itself? Silent. Unassuming. Unspectacular. Untrendy. Isn't character best when it's just doing its job, keeping its head down, maintaining consistency, not trying to be flashy or anything? Integrity, the Bible says, is something that happens within the "inner self." God reveals His wisdom and standards to us "deep within" (Ps. 51:6). His guidelines are not meant to impress but just to be faithfully pursued.

So as I start spelling out these character strengths in the remaining chapters of the book, you'll see that what makes them special is not that no one's ever thought of them before. What makes them special is that so few people ever really live them. Because when we do—when these promising traits actually begin taking the shape of flesh and bone, not just letters and syllables—guess what, they don't go unnoticed anymore. They change things. They break old habits. They demolish obstacles. They improve attitudes. They spark new beginnings. They rouse other people to action. In time they not only transform *us* but can even transform the whole culture of the places where we work and live. They are setups to a pattern of steady, sustained victory.

Sure, they may look passive at first glance, but they are powerful when set in motion.

Commitment.

Accountability.

Responsibility.

Discipline.

Sacrifice.

I believe these to be the five essential elements of a winning character.

And if it helps, you can try remembering them this way: C-A-R-D-S.

Now before we go any further, I sure hope you don't think I forced the first letters of this list so they would spell out a memorable word like that. Somebody else, in fact, was actually the first one to notice and point it out to me. The whole C-A-R-D-S thing was honestly just a happy accident.

But like I said, I had learned from long experience that these five specific building blocks of character were a crucial part of becoming a winner. If I could get my team to develop these traits and keep growing in that direction, I knew we had a good chance to win a lot of ball games. If not—well . . .

I was determined not to find that out.

So even during that first meeting with my Tulane team back in December of '96, before we'd talked about anything else, I started delivering challenges to my new players, based on the kind of character I wanted them to acquire. No, I didn't expect all of them to be enthusiastic about it—or even to stick around for it. Some of them, I figured, wouldn't be interested in putting forth the effort to adapt to a new coach and a new way of doing things. The guys who had grown comfortable with the status quo—happy being football players, even if they weren't *winning* football players—might find my style a little more direct than they wanted to deal with. And they had my full permission to bail if they didn't want in.

But I told them all (as I mentioned to you before) that for the next few weeks, neither I nor their other coaches would be around much to keep an eye on them or to give them orders about what they ought to be doing. Their own near future needed to be occupied with their final exams, then heading home for Christmas (unlike this time next year, I said, when they could count on the fact that we'd be game-planning for postseason play). With this goal in mind, in fact, the entire coaching staff would be leaving the next day or two to start scouting some new talent to come in and reinforce the future of this football program. In the meantime, however, I was expecting something specific from the guys who were already sitting there in the room with me.

First, I was expecting *accountability*. I wanted them in class, doing their work, attending everything they were supposed to show up for, performing at the highest level possible. Being accountable to their studies and their teachers was the same thing as being accountable to me and their other teammates.

I was also expecting *responsibility*. I didn't want to read their names in the newspaper, for example, discovering that they'd made some bad choices with the time on their hands, abusing the freedom of being out of school for the holidays. They were still responsible to me for being good citizens, even if that conflicted with what they thought should happen on New Year's Eve.

Add to that the *discipline* aspect of controlling their behavior, avoiding distractions, keeping themselves in reasonable health and good shape. Those were the talking points that basically summed up my directive to them for the time being, for that particular December.

Because before they knew it, Christmas break would be behind them. Mama's cooking would be a fading, fattening memory. And their new football coaches would be temporarily blocked during that part of the year from roaming the country recruiting, thanks to standard NCAA rules.

We'd be back, in other words.

And they'd better be ready. Ready to build a couple of more new character muscles to go along with the three I'd already instructed them to exercise between now and January—between now and 5:30 on a soon-and-very-soon Louisiana winter morning.

Off season conditioning is not for the faint of heart. It's early. And often. And awful. It means rolling out of the rack every day before sunrise, trudging sleepily across an otherwise quiet campus, and receiving for your brave efforts an open door to the weight room, the running track, or the various torture implements lying around on the floor mat—whatever happens to be the strength coach's personalized weapon of choice for the day.

"You *will* be challenged," I told them when that time of year rolled around. "You'll be challenged physically, mentally, every way you can think of." It was going to require a lot from them. I was clear about that.

It was going to take *commitment*.

And it was going to take *sacrifice*.

Commitment to endure the painful routine, the screaming voice in your ear, the one extra set of reps, the last half-mile, the next day—the next, the next, and the next. *Sacrifice*, too—sacrifice to your late-night social life, sacrifice to the snooze button on your alarm clock, sacrifice to so much of what others around you get to enjoy and take for granted as college students.

Trust me, I wasn't pulling my punches with anybody.

My C-A-R-D-S were all out there on the table.

But I wasn't doing it to punish. It may have sounded like I was spoiling their fun and interfering with their body's need for sleep. But in reality I was actually offering them something way better in return.

I was offering them clean, showered rides home on a Saturday evening with a winner's smile on their faces.

I was offering them a fourth-quarter burst of energy, just enough to stretch a punting situation into a first down, a sack into a scramble for positive yards, a moral victory into an actual, measurable "W"—the kind that leads to bowl games, not just head games.

I was offering them the chance to bring the crowd to its feet, the fans to the airport, and real accomplishment to their lives.

It wasn't going to be easy. But it *was* going to be attainable . . . with commitment, accountability, responsibility, discipline, and sacrifice.

We were about to counteract nearly twenty years of consistent, contagious losing and build for ourselves a winning season—and more—not only with the legs and arms of smart football players but on the strong back and shoulders of *character*.

Leading with Your Strengths

Billy Graham said it well when he talked about the "moral meltdown" that has afflicted our nation. He said the main reason behind this "tragic" turn of events is a "lack of leadership," which he went on to say is inevitably what happens when we think we can "divorce character from leadership."

The difference, as always, is character.

You cannot succeed *in anything* without it.

I knew who I wanted to be as a leader. And I knew my job as head coach was to develop leaders on my team—young men who would take their roles seriously, both on and off the field, men who would push themselves beyond the limits of their own comfort and selfishness, and who as a result would earn the clout to inspire those around them to excellence—to keep hustling, keep going, keep their focus, keep driving.

That's what I want this book to be for you, as well.

Because whether you like it or not, you are in a leadership position. As a husband, as a father, you're a leader. If you're a wife and mother, you're a leader. Even as an employee, or a student, a church member or a neighbor, you can make a daily difference in the lives of those around you. But not if you don't add to your inescapable role as *leader* the key ingredient of *character*.

I've seen these five essentials work. I've seen them lead to tangible success. I've seen them turn rowdy teenage ball players into cohesive, law-abiding, head-turning examples of raw determination. Young men with no compromise.

And I've also seen them change me—which is no small undertaking.

So I am completely confident that whatever field of endeavor you find yourself in, these five principles will make you more productive, more engaged, and more influential. They will draw you back to what matters most, while also drawing you out of yourself and your comfort zone. Connect them to Christian faith and the enabling power of the Holy Spirit within you, and there's no end to what He can make happen in your life.

Commitment.

Accountability.

Responsibility.

Discipline.

Sacrifice.

Play your C-A-R-D-S right, and I guarantee you . . . you will win.

5

Commitment

If I asked you to identify for me your top priorities in life, you'd likely answer with some variation of this simple list: *Faith, Family, and (fill in the blank)*. It's a familiar way for us to rank our main loves, values, and interests.

Yours, for example, might be faith, family, and friends.

Or faith, family, and music.

Faith, family, and church.

Faith, family, and . . . hunting. (I don't know.)

Or perhaps same as mine: faith, family, and football.

Whatever your job, or hobby, or favorite weekend pastime, that's probably the word you'd add to the list.

Faith, family, and _____.

What's yours?

The irony of this whole thing, however, is that the hardest question to answer is not what word you decide to put in the blank. The hardest question for most of us to deal with is how we can so casually and confidently say that "faith" absolutely, automatically occupies first place in our overall list of priorities. After all, there's a good chance—if we're being open and honest with ourselves—that whatever we put into that last blank is what's really our number-*one* priority: work, golf, sports, social life, whatever. "Faith" too often appears first in that list just because we know it *should*, not because it actually does.

I know. I've had to wonder that myself.

One summer several years ago, when I was in my early forties, this question kept bubbling up in my mind. I was the offensive coordinator at Auburn University at the time and was known as a Christian coach by reputation and hopefully by example. I'd already been doing a lot of faith-based speaking by then—and was doing even *more* of it every chance I got. So I was fairly active in going around telling people that my main things in life were "faith, family, and football"—in that order. Felt good saying it that way.

But let me tell you why I wasn't so sure it was true, the more I thought about it.

I knew football every way a man can know it. Front ways and back ways. Offense, defense, special teams. Technique, footwork, passing routes, everything. I'd studied it. I'd played it. I'd coached hundreds of guys in it. I'm not saying there's no better football mind in the world than my own, of course. But I had been around the sport for so long, and I'd obviously learned it from one of the best *ever* in my father. So let's just say there's probably not a single football subject you could bring up that I wouldn't at least have a strong opinion on—and probably a few firsthand examples and observations to support my belief.

And, hey, there's nothing wrong with knowing that much about football, any more than there's anything wrong with you knowing as much as you do about your own line of work or your particular field of study. Football's a lot of fun for most people, it's a regular topic of conversation, and it's a big part of life for those who've chosen it as a profession. I would never have enjoyed the success I had in coaching if I hadn't known football inside and out.

But, still . . . that's how much I said I knew about my *third highest priority* in life.

Third.

How much did I know about my *first?*

I dare you to sit on that question a while.

Time for a Change

The first thing to understand about *commitment*—maybe the *only* thing we need to understand about it—is its basic, one-to-one relationship with *time*. If you really want to know where your true commitment lies, just see where you're spending the bulk of your waking hours.

Now obviously I know our jobs take the largest actual chunk out of every day, week, and month. We can't help that. And the truth is, we're commanded by God Himself to "labor six days and do all [our] work" (Exod. 20:9), only being sure to take a Sabbath rest each week for worship and refreshment.

Work is good, not a curse, as some people believe. Back at the beginning of creation, before sin had ever entered the world, "the LORD God took the man [Adam] and placed him in the garden of Eden to *work it* and watch over it" (Gen. 2:15).

So commitment to our work and our commitment to Christ are not mutually exclusive, as though you have to choose one or the other, as if you can't do both at the same time. You don't have to wait till your workday is over before you can put on your Christian hat and do Christian things. They're designed to be all incorporated into one big package of integrity, diligence, and faithfulness. God is pleased by that.

So I'm not saying you're necessarily an out-of-balance workaholic, married more to your job than you are to your spouse, just because most of your measurable time is invested in the day's business. I'm just asking—if you're someone like me who says with your mouth that "faith" and all it entails is your top priority—then what kind of *time* are you setting aside to cultivate it?

- How would anyone know that you're committed to it?
- How do you know in your own heart that you're dedicated to it?
- What's different about the way you order your day and week because of it?
- How much of a *time commitment* do you give to your faith?

That's what I felt like the Lord was asking me.

And I only knew one place to go to find an answer.

Gospel Truth

The Bible is not actually just a book. It is a "book of books," meaning it's like its own library, composed of sixty-six individual volumes housed inside one cover, written by forty different authors. (Whenever I'd share that little Bible fact with my football players—which a coach can do when he shuts the door to his own locker room—I could always see a few of those big defensive linemen scratching their heads and looking at me funny. I'd say, "Guys, that just means some of 'em wrote more than one book, OK?" They could never seem to figure that part out.)

A lot of people think the Bible is a bunch of fairy tales, made up for the purpose of guilting us into obedience to this invisible God, who probably just wants our money or something. But the apostle Peter, one of Jesus' closest disciples—and author of two books in the New Testament—came right out and said, "We did not follow cleverly contrived myths when we made known to you the power and coming of our Lord Jesus Christ; instead, we were eyewitnesses of His majesty" (2 Pet. 1:16). Then referring back to the writers of the Old Testament, he said, "No prophecy ever came by the will of man; instead men spoke from God as they were moved by the Holy Spirit" (v. 21).

These were not fables they were spinning; this was God's Word in real life, things they had seen and could testify to, things they had heard from His mouth. Many, like Peter, were forced to back up their bold statements by being imprisoned, tortured, and ultimately killed for their faith, including most all of Jesus' other apostles, as well as many hundreds more of His followers down through the years—down to this very day, in fact.

That's a high cost to pay for defending a lie.

But that's certainly not the only skeptical complaint people have about the Scriptures. Others, for example, think there's just no way the Bible can be verified as authentic and trustworthy. Who's to say it can back up its claims? There's not an original sample available for us to see, they argue, to prove it's legitimate. Yet upwards of twenty-five thousand different man-uscripts, excerpts, and documents have been unearthed—cen-turies old—providing a mountain of evidence to support the genuineness of the Bible text, far more proof than exists for the writings of people like Homer and Shakespeare, works whose authenticity is accepted flat-out without a second thought.

In the hundreds of years since God's Word was first duplicated on the printing press—a feat for which a whole new wave of believers spilled their life's blood in defending its distribution—the Bible has been a continual best seller across all generational and cultural lines. It's been translated into more than two thousand languages, and it's now available in just about every format and book binding imaginable. You can carry it under your arm, in your pocket, or even on your telephone.

That's our Bible.

You've probably got one near your desk, another at your bedside, another in your car, another one or two or three on your bookshelf.

So did I.

I mean, would you expect any less from a well-known Christian man? From a guy who said his "faith" was his top priority? Of course not.

But when the Lord got hold of me that summer, when I was doing all that speaking to men's groups, and church groups, and Fellowship of Christian Athletes events, I had to ask myself: What gave me the right to stand up there and tell people how important my faith was to me, when I hadn't read all the way through the Bible *even one time!*

The most important book in the history of mankind. The one book that offers answers to the most challenging questions of life. The one book that claims to be the very Word of God for His people—inerrant (without error), infallible (without falsehood), literally what the Lord Himself has chosen to reveal to us about His nature, His character, and His plan for our lives.

Count it up: more than two thousand times in the pages of that book, its many writers wrote the words "thus saith the Lord" or some equivalent phrase. And all I'd ever done for the first forty some-odd years of my life was just to read it hit and miss? Here and there? Even though I'd devoured dozens of books throughout that time on football, coaching, and strategy.

What's wrong with this picture?

Is the same thing wrong with yours?

Commitment Level

I'm telling you, it convicted me. It challenged my *commitment* level. And I made up my mind I was going to do something about it.

I promised God I would start devoting myself to His Word.

Oh, sure, I had *read* it. I'd dipped into and out of it. I'd followed along with it in my lap a thousand times while the pastor preached his sermon. I'd even told a lot of its stories and general ideas to my kids through the years. I considered myself fairly familiar with the Bible—and was!

But *committed* to it? Committed to learning it, hearing from God through it, being changed by it?

Not so much.

My so-called number one priority.

So here's what I did. My mother-in-law had given us a really nice study Bible, one with a lot of notes and commentary at the bottom of each page. It wasn't presented in an over-the-top scholarly way. They'd designed the study helps to be easy to understand by an ordinary person. But it was extensive. A big book. The whole Scripture was in there, of course, but then it gave lots of verse-by-verse insights on biblical themes, explained what various things meant, laid out time lines and historical frameworks, really pulled you into the meat of the experience.

This wasn't just Bible *reading*. It was Bible *study*.

And I started at the beginning. Genesis 1:1. Went through every verse. Read every note and comment and text box and call-out. I started off at thirty minutes a day, first thing in the morning—reading, pondering, praying about what God was showing me. Then I went to forty-five minutes. Then an hour.

And five and a half years later—yes, about a month per Bible book from the time I started—I had finally worked my way to the back cover.

Now, listen, that's not because I'm a slow reader. (I went to West Virginia University, after all. Come on.) But God had given me a burden for knowing Him and His Word, the same way I knew football—backward and forward, A to Z, sunup to sundown. And in five and a half years' time, He rewarded my commitment by showing me over and over and over again, one day after another, that "all the treasures of wisdom and knowledge are hidden in Him" (Col. 2:3).

It's all right there. In His Word.

For those who are *committed* to meeting Him in it.

I don't know how to quantify exactly the many benefits God has given me as a result of pursuing a deeper encounter with Him through His Word, the Bible. It wasn't just that one time, either. When I'd finished making my first complete pass from front to back, I started all over again and was able to make it through a little more quickly—just *four* and a half years this time. Then I started again and shaved it to *three* and a half years. I'm now on my fourth time through, using other kinds of study materials, of course, to give me a little different experience. It's been more than fifteen years altogether since I first began. He's shown me so much.

But I can tell you this for sure. The December after I made that new commitment to learning God's Word was when I got the phone call asking if I'd be interested in talking with the athletic department at Tulane about their head coaching position. And the renewed depth of relationship God had allowed me to develop with Him over the course of those few months provided me with a level of clarity and peace He must've known I would need for being ready to make that decision. Taking on a new, exposed role like that can be as daunting for a man as it is desirable. It is nothing if not overwhelming. But by helping me put "faith" first, where it had always belonged, He enabled me to feel spiritually confident about moving forward.

Commitment to God had given me assurance not only in my football instincts and abilities but also in His will and His perfect timing, which is really what matters most of all.

First Things First

I'm challenging you today to come clean on your priorities, the way God challenged me fifteen years ago—and still challenges me every day. I'm asking you to make a commitment of your *time* to what you say means more to you than anything.

And I'm encouraging you to start first thing in the morning.

I don't know what I'd have done if I hadn't.

People often ask me what it's like being a college football coach. And my initial, gut-response answer is to try to dispel the myth that college coaching is a seasonal job—that it cranks up in late summer and then ends, if you're lucky, around New Year's Day. The truth is, it's year-round. And on average it's around one hundred hours a week. Often more.

I would usually be in my office at or before 6:00 a.m. on a typical day, and I wouldn't leave till around 9:00 that night. Fifteen hours a day. But during the heavy recruiting season, despite the fact that I was able to use a private plane to travel from place to place, even having on-call transportation didn't usually prevent me from getting back home before 11:00, 12:00, 1:00 in the morning—or to keep 6:30 from still being the hard start-of-business next day. If we had a road game someplace—like Texas, for example, an 8:00 national telecast—the game would be over a little after 11:00, we'd do our interviews and wrap-up, shower and drive to the airport, work our way through security, and maybe be home by 4:00 a.m.

Such is life.

And yes, we love it. And get paid well for it.

But then in the off season—

Wait, *what* off season? Ask my wife if there's any such thing as an *off season*. I mean, recruiting never stops, of course. As head coach, I was also responsible for speaking to various groups and venues to raise money for the university, not to mention my own public speaking to faith-based audiences.

Spring practice was never too far around the corner, then football camps, then meetings, then media obligations. Summer was as light as it ever got, when for about two weeks I could keep it to an eight-hour workday—"vacation" for a college football coach.

So it's obviously intense. Nonstop.

But it reminds me of a quote that's generally attributed to the great Christian reformer Martin Luther. Whether he actually said it or not, I don't know, but the sentiment is true nonetheless. He once claimed that his days were becoming so full, crowded with so many things to accomplish, he felt compelled to—what? Hustle a little faster through his prayer time so he could knuckle down to business quicker? No. He was so overwhelmed by his responsibilities, he felt compelled to *increase* his prayer time in the morning . . . from two hours to three. Otherwise, he knew he'd never make it.

Now I'm no Martin Luther, naturally, but I know where he's coming from. The temptation is to think, *Hey, I'm way too busy to stop and read the Bible or do my devotions. I've barely got time to brush my teeth in the morning!* Spiritual disciplines are usually the first place to cut whenever there's a time crunch. But for me, I knew I couldn't make it through a schedule like mine unless I showed up at the office early, before everybody else, and spent at least a half hour (usually more) reading my Bible, getting quiet with God, just letting Him set my mind on Him in preparation for the day ahead.

I might be scheduled to meet later in the morning with the athletic director. I might find out at some point in the day that one of my players had been caught overnight with drugs in his possession. I might encounter a disagreement with one of the coaches on my staff over a game-planning decision or a judgment call of some kind. Any number of things could crop up. Or I might simply just not feel like being there that day, whether from fatigue or family concerns or lazy effort by my football team at practice.

But if I had been faithfully committed to my first priority, I only had to look back as far as that morning, to the dim, dawning hours of that day, to remember what God had promised me in His Word such a short time ago—that He'd never "leave" me or "forsake" me (Josh. 1:5), that I could trust Him to be my "strength and my shield" (Ps. 28:7), that He would be faithful to "teach me good judgment and discernment" (Ps. 119:66), that He would give me "such words and a wisdom that none of your adversaries will be able to resist or contradict" (Luke 21:15).

I had taken *time* to be with God, first thing, right off the bat. And that commitment was still coloring my day—even when my day was still in motion way past dinner time that night.

That's just how it needs to be.

That's how you succeed.

It takes *commitment*.

But if you'll begin there—doesn't have to be an hour or more, could be way less, given your circumstances and situation—if you'll commit to starting your day with God, you'll start seeing yourself making better decisions. All day long—before you go into that next meeting, before you make an important phone call, before you're tasked with reprimanding an employee, or apologizing to a client, or correcting one of your children—you'll feel close enough to God from your growing relationship with Him that you can pull the door closed for thirty seconds and pray about what He wants you to do.

It's just one of the blessings of commitment.

It's what happens when faith takes first place.

Lasting Commitment

This feels like a good time to peel back for a second and just make sure we're all on the same page.

A lot of people talk about having faith and placing a high importance on that particular aspect of their lives. That's good. But there are many different definitions out there for *faith*, and not all of them are able to anchor us in a place where it's safe to live.

People can hope and dream for things all they want to. That's faith of a sort. They can believe, despite what they see with their eyes, that there's a purpose behind what they're being forced to endure. That takes faith as well. But faith alone—having faith in your faith—doesn't really do much for you. It might help you keep a stiff chin and a determined smile on your face, but that kind of faith can only take you so far.

Faith by itself is not where your true strength lies. The much stronger side of the equation is the part that tells you what your faith is *in*. And if your faith is in Jesus Christ—who came to Earth as both God and man, lived a pure and spotless life, then offered Himself willingly on the cross, becoming the only acceptable sacrifice that could ever pay the full penalty for your sins and mine—only then is your faith truly worth something.

When your faith is in the incomparable power of the resurrected Christ, it doesn't have to be any bigger than "the size of a mustard seed" to be able to "tell this mountain, 'Move from here to there,' and it will move. Nothing will be impossible for you" (Matt. 17:20)—not merely because you believe it, but because "the One who is in you is greater than the one who is in the world" (1 John 4:4).

Oh, I know I'm most likely preaching to the choir here. You've probably received Christ as Savior already, and you're following Him as Lord the best you know how. But if not—if you're not really sure that you've ever surrendered control of your life, your hopes, and your eternal destiny into God's loving, capable hands—Jesus is right here in this moment to take you there.

Yes, it's hard in some ways to admit we're sinners who have fallen short of the glory of God (Rom. 3:23), that we need Someone else to do for us what we can't do for ourselves. It's not easy to hear that the "wages of sin"—the ultimate payment for clinging to our selfish ways and desires—is "death" (Rom. 6:23).

But God "proves His own love for us in that while we were still sinners, Christ died for us" (Rom. 5:8). "For God did not send His Son into the world that He might condemn the world, but that the world might be saved through Him" (John 3:17).

So, really, like I've said before, it's simple. "If you confess with your mouth, 'Jesus is Lord,' and believe in your heart that God raised Him from the dead, you will be saved. For everyone who calls on the name of the Lord will be saved" (Rom. 10:9, 13). "And if the Spirit of Him who raised Jesus from the dead lives in you, then He who raised Christ from the dead will also bring your mortal bodies to life through His Spirit" (Rom. 8:11).

That's the strong commitment God has made to you.

What kind of commitment have you made to Him?

When I talk about *faith* (in the "faith, family, and football" sense), I'm talking about faith in Jesus Christ that turns weak, prideful, ambitious, self-absorbed people like us into men and women who can be used of God to impact the world for His honor and glory—people who can become models of stability, strength, and consistency because of the One who has made a way to change us.

Be committed to *that*—committed to *Him*—and you've nailed down the first, essential plank in a solid foundation for lasting success.

You've truly put first things first.

6

Accountability

obody else does it quite the same.

N   Before every kickoff at Clemson University's Memorial Stadium ("Death Valley," to those who've experienced the competitive environment there for themselves), the players depart their dressing room under the stands in the west end zone, board two charter buses, and are then accompanied by loud, blaring, full-siren police escort halfway around the stadium before being dropped off at the hill behind the *east* end zone, high atop the playing surface.

Howard's Rock is up there, just inside the seating area—a gift to legendary coach Frank Howard from a Clemson alum who snatched it from the hot sands of the *real* Death Valley in eastern California. Every fall since the 1967 season, thousands of game-day ballplayers have rubbed that stone on their way into the stadium, seeking to invoke the magic of football glory. It remains part of what makes this moment so nostalgic and special.

With the supercharged roar of the stadium basically at their *feet*—imagine that—the players lunge and retreat like caged animals, held back by coaches and team assistants, hardly able to stand in one place. Then, finally—in what ESPN broadcaster Brent Musburger has called "the most exciting twenty-five seconds in college football"—the marching band cycles into their two-line formation down at field level, the cannon booms, the players bolt, the crowd erupts, and a huge, flapping, tiger-paw flag leads the orange charge down the hill, surrounded on both sides by screaming fans— from the top row of the bleachers to the base of the goalpost— before disbursing in a mass toward the home team sideline. It's a frenzy of "Tiger Rag" mania and mayhem. It's another reason college football stirs your blood and makes you wish it was Saturday.

Do yourself a favor. Go sometime.

But every now and then, caught up in a moment filled with such high emotion—like at any college stadium on any given game day—people don't always channel their release of pent-up energy in the right direction. Maybe you've been in certain situations yourself—perhaps at home, or at work, or in some public setting—where the tension built to a peak level, and you overreacted to what you were feeling. You did something that was out of place and out of character. You lashed out at somebody. You said something you should never have said. You lost your temper and couldn't seem to rein it in before you had caused significant damage. That's what happens when we don't keep ourselves under control, when we don't choose to direct the force of all that volatile emotion in a positive, constructive fashion.

And that's what happened on November 20, 2004—the last game of the regular season, against archrival South Carolina—when the run down the hill became a run-in with trouble.

A number of unfortunate circumstances contributed to the events of that afternoon. First, the officiating crew that was assigned to the game was from the Southeastern Conference and was not as familiar with the unique dynamics of Clemson's pregame ritual. The ACC referees who work those games all the time are always careful to keep the opposing players from being anywhere within twenty-five yards of the end zone whenever the home team is taking the field. On this particular day, however, several of the Gamecock players were waiting at the bottom of the hill, taunting our guys, taking a few swings, inciting a reaction.

Second, Coach Lou Holtz had told his team unofficially the previous Thursday that he would be retiring at the end of the season. The formal announcement wouldn't be made until the following Monday, but everyone pretty much knew what was going on. So the South Carolina team was beginning to deal with impending change, and I'm sure they were already feeling some of the lack of structure that often goes along with situations like that.

Third—even though some people didn't want to believe this incident had any effect—a professional basketball game between the Detroit Pistons and Indiana Pacers the night before had been interrupted by a wild, bench-clearing altercation that ended up with players jumping into the stands, slugging at fans who had thrown cups and concession debris toward the basketball court. (You probably remember it. One of the players, Ron Artest, was suspended without pay for the rest of the season. Several others received significant penalties. It was truly historic.) The scene was played and replayed on sports channels and highlight clips around the clock, and it was naturally a big part of what the nineteen- and twenty-year-olds who play college football on Saturday afternoon had been watching on TV in their dorm rooms and apartments all Friday night.

Still . . .

Everyone who participated in the pushing and shoving that took place before kickoff, as well as the larger brawl that broke out midway through the fourth quarter, was entirely responsible for his own behavior. No amount of excuses or justifications offset the fact that the players who were directly involved—on both teams—were way out of line. Most of the people on the field were out there trying to pull other players off, to get them away from the fighting. But nobody needed to be fighting in the first place.

And for that both teams were held *accountable*.

I'll be honest, I felt like the penalty that was worked out between the administrations of both schools was too harsh. Not being allowed to accept a hard-earned bowl invitation ended up costing each of my players—many of whom came from poor socioeconomic backgrounds—the opportunity to receive up to $2,000 in gifts and cash payments from the bowl organizations. (That amount of money would've come in mighty handy to them and their families at Christmastime.) My coaches and I were also denied bonuses that I hated for them not to receive after all the work they'd put in through-out the season.

I supported the decision publicly because I didn't want to be seen as endorsing or minimizing what had happened on the field. I promised the president and AD that I'd be a company man. Inside, however, I felt as though a more equitable solution would have been to hand out isolated sus-pensions to the players who were most at fault rather than to penalize the entire team as well as our faithful fans and ticket holders.

But you know what? We don't always get to choose the consequences of our actions, even the ones we may only be indirectly involved in—guilt by association—even the ones that are committed not by us personally but by people for whom we are responsible, as I was.

So even though I may have felt myself bucking a little bit at what this fiasco had cost my team, my staff, and our many ardent supporters, I also knew there was a great deal of value in the lesson it taught.

Every action results in either cost or reward.

They call that . . . *accountability*.

Platform Speaking

I don't care who you are, whom you know, what you do, or what you've done. Every single one of us needs the protection of being held accountable for our actions. Environments that don't maintain a healthy check on individuals' behaviors, allowing people to get away with things unpunished, will eventually pay for it with failure. Human nature being what it is, none of us benefit from not being required to answer for the choices we make. We need other people in our lives who are willing to question and correct our poor judgment.

It makes us sharper.

It forces us to concentrate harder.

It helps us learn from our mistakes rather than repeating the same ones over and over again until they become ingrained habits.

It keeps us in position to succeed.

God, being our Creator, knows this about us. "He knows what we are made of, remembering that we are dust" (Ps. 103:14). He knows that the human heart "is more deceitful than anything else and incurable—who can understand it?" (Jer. 17:9). He knows, left to ourselves, we will almost invariably tend toward becoming slow, sloppy, and selfish. So in His great wisdom God holds us accountable for our actions, for our inactions, and for how we choose to handle the opportunities He's given us.

And we need that because we can't always count on having other people around to keep an eye on us. We like to think we can do things nobody else knows about. We're able to convince ourselves that our sins and shortcomings are not hurting anybody and that they're not really anybody else's business anyway. We all too easily become like those people described in the Psalms, who say, "How can God know? Does the Most High know everything?" (Ps. 73:11). "The LORD doesn't see it. The God of Jacob doesn't pay attention" (Ps. 94:7).

Don't kid yourself. "Whatever a man sows he will also reap," the Bible says (Gal. 6:7). There's no squeezing around this immovable principle.

Because even if we appear to be getting off scot-free today with our poor decisions and unwatched behavior, at some point in the future "we must all appear before the tribunal of Christ, so that each may be repaid for what he has done in the body, whether good or worthless" (2 Cor. 5:10).

So this is serious business.

Don't take *accountability* lightly.

As Christians, of course, we can be confident that our sins—even the ones we haven't thought of or committed yet—are completely forgiven because of our faith in the finished work of Christ. As the Bible says, "If we confess our sins, He is faithful and righteous to forgive us our sins and to cleanse us from all unrighteousness" (1 John 1:9).

But even this comforting fact does not keep us from being accountable for what we do with what we've been given. The Bible is a true story of grace and mercy, of love and redemption, but it also contains a strong message of accountability, and no one is exempt from it. "When a righteous person turns from his righteousness and commits iniquity, he will die on account of this. But when a wicked person turns from his wickedness and does what is just and right, he will live because of this" (Ezek. 33:18–19).

So when I die, I know I'm going to heaven. That's the promise of salvation. When the Lord opens the "book of life" (as mentioned in Rev. 20:12), my name is sure to be listed there. Tommy Bowden. I hope yours is too. But I don't believe that's the only thing God will mention to me when I stand before Him in judgment. I believe He'll remind me, for example, that He allowed me to become a head coach in 1996 and continued to provide me with that position and platform for the next twelve years. During each of those seasons, a hundred guys sat there in my locker room and participated on my practice field. Each one of them looked to me as an authority figure. They depended on me for instruction, for guidance, for advice, and for playing time. *So let me ask you, Tommy Bowden, did they see a difference in you because of your faith in Christ—what you claimed to be your number one priority?* Did I use the opportunity to introduce them to my Savior? Did I care more about their souls than their playing ability? Or was I too afraid of the ACLU to talk about anything else but football while I had their ear and attention?

No, that's not going to keep me out of heaven.

But I *will* be held accountable for it.

And you—what's the God-given platform *you've* been allowed to stand on and declare the truth of Christ?

- How have you handled the privilege of being your wife's husband, for example, treating her with an unselfish, unconditional love, modeling for her the kind of devotion God has directed toward you, even when *you* don't deserve it?
- How have you managed your household and instructed your children, showing them God's principles in action—behind closed doors, in real life?
- How have you performed your work and carried yourself at the office, the factory, the job site, the classroom? What kinds of conversations have you had

with the other people around you? What have you laughed at and participated in?

- How have you responded to success? Have you allowed it to go to your head, leading you to treat others as if they're not in your league?
- How have you reacted to failure or disappointment? Would others know from your demeanor that you serve a Lord and Savior worthy of your complete trust and confidence, even when you're going through difficult situations?

You and I have each been given certain platforms, and we have done whatever we've done with them—with each of those daily opportunities. We continue to do whatever we're doing with them now.

And like it or not, we will be held accountable for that.

We should expect no less.

Accountability Hits Home

One area I want to address specifically in discussing accountability is the role of parents. Particularly fathers. As dads, we are going to be held accountable—more than our wives are—for the way we have led, loved, and counseled our children. Not everybody likes the way this sounds, but the Bible is crystal clear about it: we husbands are the "head" of our wives and families (Eph. 5:23). He has placed us in charge of the spiritual growth and development of our kids.

Sure, the pastor certainly plays an important role in this, as do other members of the church body and ministerial staff, teachers, as well as the various authority figures in our children's lives—grandparents, adult family friends, and close relatives. Each of these people can help. But if we expect our sons and daughters to grow spiritually as they age, if we want them to be discipled well in the Christian faith, it is not up to all those other people to do it. Truth is, it's more on us than on anybody else.

We—not our wives—will be held most accountable.

Listen, I understand why a lot of us don't feel qualified for such a daunting challenge. I was raised in a Christian home where I learned biblical truth from my father's words as well as his actions. Yet I still felt inadequate in being prepared and committed to this task. I can only imagine what it's like for those men who never saw it modeled for them at home when they were children themselves. Maybe *you* are one of those people.

I think back to a sizable number of the guys I recruited as a college football coach. I can't tell you how many homes I visited that were led by single moms working two or three jobs to keep the lights on and the grocery bills paid. A lot of the young athletes I recruited would come home from school and ball practice every evening to an empty house, fix their own meager meals, and go to bed under a roof with no father in the house, same as every other night. It's hard to see how kids growing up with that kind of lifestyle and perspective would ever be able to mature into responsible fathers who are engaged in their children's spiritual lives, having had no first-hand concept of what that experience even means.

But the inner city is not the only place where this lack occurs. Given the state of far too many of our families today—even those with money and fine homes and all the appearances of success—I'd say there's a good chance that you, too, didn't have an upbringing that truly equipped you to know what all was expected of you as a father when you finally had children of your own.

But I'm here to tell you, you don't have to be a degreed theologian to instruct your children in the ways of God—not that there's anything undesirable about having advanced religious training. I'm certainly not meaning to make light of guys who are highly educated, as if that somehow makes them less of a "real man." I'm just saying that it doesn't matter how much or how little you know, or how much or how little you've received—you can still begin where you are, confident that God will use even your stumbling attempts at spiritual teaching to produce unmistakable fruit in your children's lives.

Just because you don't know exactly what to do doesn't mean you're not held accountable for doing it.

Nobody could have started much more simply than I did with my own children. I was twenty-seven years old when our first child was born, and three years later our second one came along. I can remember sitting down with Ryan and Lauren when they were just one and four, opening up a Bible story-book that had a big picture on one side and a short retelling of the story on the other.

I'm talking about Adam and Eve, Noah and the ark, Daniel and the lion's den, Samson and Delilah, Joseph and his coat of many colors. I would read one story at a time, point out various little things in the picture, and just generally try to explain to them what was going on.

As they got older, we'd read chapters from the Bible— just like that, no other book or resource required—usually from the life of Christ or from the later books of the New Testament, perhaps from Psalms or Proverbs, and then we'd just discuss what it said. Nobody understands *everything* that's embedded there, of course—all the deep shades of meaning and application—but anyone, to the best of their ability, can share what a particular verse seems to be saying or instructing them to do.

Then we'd pray together, thanking God for His blessings, asking for His help in school and work, always mentioning people we knew who were dealing with particular needs. I'd ask my kids to pray, too, just so they could get in the habit of being comfortable talking with God. I didn't want the only prayers they heard or participated in to be the ones we said before dinner and at bedtime.

What I'm saying, men, is that it's not really all that hard when you think about it. The hard part is just making it important enough in our minds and in our schedules—putting *faith* high enough on our actual, real-life priority list—that we become intentional about leading our children into relationship with God through His Word and through a commitment to meeting with Him together on a regular basis.

That's what the Bible means when it tells parents to talk about Him "when you sit in your house and when you walk along the road, when you lie down and when you get up" (Deut. 6:7). We're not supposed to "hide" these things from our children but instead to "tell a future generation the praises of the LORD, His might, and the wonderful works He has performed . . . so that they might put their confidence in God and not forget God's works, but keep His commands" (Ps. 78:4, 7).

Sure, they could read the Bible themselves. And we certainly ought to encourage them to do so as they get older. But think about it: *your* name is not in the Bible. What God has done and is doing in *your* life is not something they'll ever find out about by reading the Bible alone. They need to hear you give personal testimony to how those words on the page are taking shape in real time. No one else can tell them how God is working in your family, in ways that can only be explained by His direct involvement and His deep love for each one of you.

And if for some reason this doesn't feel important enough to drag you away from your desk or the computer or a basketball game on television, maybe this one little reminder will help.

You are accountable to God for it.

You can expect a cost—or a reward—depending on how you've invested yourself in this crucial area of your life.

My children are grown and gone now. I'm not able to see them all the time. But every now and then, at special seasons when we're together over holidays or on vacation, I'm still able to sit down with them and share the Scriptures, talk about the blessings of God on our family, and pray with them in real, genuine, authentic ways.

You can't put a value on that kind of freedom and access to your children's hearts.

But I hurt for fathers who are paying the price for being too afraid, too preoccupied—too whatever—to take an active role in their children's spiritual lives. Any old excuse will work when you don't really want to do something. But you can end up nursing a lot of old regrets when your children grow up not showing much interest in following Christ, when they haven't been deliberately taught how to restrain themselves under His authority.

I know I'm touching on a tender spot whenever I talk to men about this. In your case, perhaps, it may feel "too little too late" to do much about it. You feel like you've squandered all your opportunities. You don't know how to redeploy your energies now to make any difference.

Or maybe you didn't come to Christ until later in life, or didn't get serious about living for Him until only recently. You honestly didn't know any better when your kids were young, when you had more of an opening into their lives.

And, yes, it's easier to catch them young. If you're still in your twenties without any children yet or with small kids at home, I urge you to make that commitment now. Share the Scriptures with them. Tell them the great stories of the Bible. Pray with them every chance you get, and try as hard as you can to model the heavenly Father you're pointing them toward.

But even if your children are older, trust God for the opportunity to restore what you didn't do earlier. Ask your kids' forgiveness for not being more devoted to helping them grow in their faith. Try hard to reestablish spiritual connections with them—even your adult children. Look for ways as a grandfather (if that's where you are) to plant Christian truth into the lives of your grandkids.

One thing you learn in football is that you can't do anything about the last play. Even if your mistake or turnover led directly to points for the other team, all you can do now is play harder and smarter on the next one. Coaches teach their players to have short memories.

So I urge you to receive God's mercy for what you didn't do as a young father. Let go of the guilt, knowing it will only keep you feeling tentative and cautious, afraid to exert your best efforts now. Then seek whatever inroads still remain into your children's hearts.

It's not too late to turn this into something positive.

In fact, you're being held accountable for that.

Iron Sharpening Iron

Accountability makes for winning football teams. Accountability makes for healthy lives, marriages, and families. Accountability creates lean, productive business environments. It draws out the best in people who would tend to slack off and give half-effort otherwise.

No, you don't need to feel accountable to everyone. If I'd thought I was accountable to every radio caller or e-mail writer who insisted I fire a certain coach, or make a quarter-back change, or spice up our third-down play calling, I would never have stopped chasing other people's expectations—often to the detriment of what was best for our football team.

But part of a winning character means knowing you will be made to answer for your actions to the people who have a legitimate right to demand it. It means not intentionally gravitating toward situations and environments where you're out from under others' scrutiny. It means realizing that your best "you" emerges only when you're held to higher standards than you'd probably enforce upon yourself.

I used to remind my players that the New Testament talks about love, mercy, forgiveness—lots of nice words like that. But if my team failed to perform on the field or in the classroom, if they didn't give me maximum effort during a practice or football game, they could expect my discipline to be *Old Testament*: an eye for an eye, a tooth for a tooth. They would be held strictly accountable for the awareness, hustle, and intensity they brought to any given situation. (Then if we won, of course, they could experience the nice *New* Testament part.)

That's just how winners win—not because they're constantly looking over their shoulder, like a puppy waiting to be smacked by a rolled-up newspaper, but because they accept the reality that their actions will come with either cost or reward. Rather than fighting the inevitable, they allow (and even invite) the presence of accountability into their lives to keep them on their toes at all times. They harness the healthy power of pressure to help mold them into people who are growing more capable and trustworthy with each passing day.

They become one of those rare men and women who are the same person in private as they are in public because they know they're not only accountable to a boss, a spouse, a coach, or a parent, but ultimately to God, who sees everything else.

None of us is above being held accountable.

And each of us is better because of it.

7

Responsibility

Pick up a newspaper nowadays, pull out the sports page, and you're nearly as likely to read about a player being hauled in on a misdemeanor charge as hauling in a game-winning touchdown.

A recent *Sports Illustrated* study chronicled police reports involving pro and college athletes—football and basketball only—for an eight-month period. And even while tossing out dozens of minor violations to keep from artificially bulging the numbers, they finally stopped counting at 125 cases of serious, jailable offenses. That's a steady clip of about one allegation every other day. Drunk driving. Bar fights. Robberies. Assault. Domestic violence. Drug possession. Attacks on girlfriends. Even weapons charges. Felonies.

And the largest category of athletes involved in these major scrapes with the law? By far?

College football players.

Surprised?

I'm not. For the greater part of my adult life, I've been in the faces of eighteen- to twenty-one-year old football players, any number of whom feel like they're bigger than the campus, bigger than the rules, and bigger than the system. It's a lot of male testosterone for coaches to account for—twenty-four hours a day, every day (and night) of the week—but that's what their coaches are all too frequently paid to do, almost as much as getting them to remember their blocking assignments.

I learned early on, however, that I could save myself a lot of time answering reporters' questions about players' off-the-field shenanigans if I could get my guys to grasp a basic yet highly important concept.

Responsibility.

And because of our staunch commitment to that, I actually had few disciplinary problems to manage as a head coach. I know from many years now of established experience that when you can get a young man to start seeing himself as being personally responsible for his behavior, you go a long way toward protecting him from his own runaway impulses.

And what's true for shifty young running backs and receivers in a rowdy college town is just as true for tire salesmen, store managers, CEOs, and X-ray technicians—every guy in every job at every age and income level imaginable. The active trait of *responsibility* is an ongoing game-changer for anyone who wants to remain on a constant trajectory toward success.

We are each responsible for ourselves and for what's been given into our care to influence and control. We each have roles to play and (as mentioned in the last chapter) a price to pay for how we handle it. The way this fleshes itself out in your own life will be somewhat different from mine, different from your friends, different from others. But the way you manage your own unique responsibilities—even on your downtime and weekends—will make a huge difference in where you're headed in life.

Take Care of Yourself

Matthew 25 is a sweeping discourse on responsibility—on its many results and ramifications, how it progresses and grows upon itself in a person's life. Everything that's said in this passage is taken directly from the mouth of Jesus. The only thing that's not printed in red letters is the chapter number. But instead of teaching with thou-shalts and shalt-nots, Jesus communicates this important life message through stories. As usual, He does more showing than telling. He illustrates it in ways we can more easily remember and put into practice.

So He starts with a parable about ten women who were waiting for the groom to arrive for a wedding banquet. The hour grew late, the groom hadn't been seen yet, and the young women who hadn't thought to bring any extra oil along to keep their lamps burning, should he be later than expected, faced a problem. They first wished the other girls would loan them some of theirs since time was probably too short to go back and find more. But just like it wasn't anybody else's job to remember their oil for them, neither was it anybody else's job to bail them out for not thinking ahead. They were the ones responsible, as well as the ones accountable. And sure enough, by the time they returned with fresh oil in hand, the groom had already shown up, started the festivities, and shut the door behind him. Their carelessness had caused them to miss out, to fail at meeting their objective.

Here's what I take from that. Any way you look at it, the main, bottom line of responsibility is being responsible for yourself. No one else is to blame if you don't take care of your own business and keep yourself focused on what you ought to be doing.

This goes for simple things. In football it means being responsible to know the snap count, to know what down it is, to know which man you're supposed to block, to know where you need to be positioned in a certain coverage, to know how many time outs are left, to know which foot to lead with, to know when an audible called at scrimmage affects your own personal assignment. Everything can fall apart in a hurry if even one member of the team is not doing his job.

We are all responsible for our own stuff. And as primitive as that may sound, we do well to remember it every morning.

We are responsible for being committed to God's Word. We are responsible for depending on Him in prayer. We are responsible for checking the air in our tires, for paying our bills on time, for maintaining a diet high in vitamins and low in french fries.

We live in a society that's always pointing the finger somewhere else—blaming our parents, blaming our teachers, blaming our government, blaming company policy, blaming everybody but ourselves for being in the fixes we're in. And while there may actually be a hint of truth in some of our complaints and contentions, nothing changes the fact that the primary person responsible for what's going right or wrong in our own lives . . . is *us*.

You'll often hear comments after a close loss, how a questionable flag cost us the game, or a teammate who dropped a catchable ball, or a bad spot by the referee that left us short of a first down and stalled a final scoring drive. But any team in a sixty-minute game is given dozens of opportunities throughout each minute of each quarter to build a victory résumé that no referee's whistle or clock malfunction should be able to overcome. Any loss ultimately boils down to a failure to execute, both individually and as a unit. Attempts to pass it off on others doesn't

just *sound* like sour grapes—*they are.*

No one enjoys consistent success without owning responsibility for himself.

Nobody.

Expanding Your Role

The second of Jesus' three stories from Matthew 25 is His well-known parable of the talents, where a wealthy landowner heads out on an extended journey, assigning several of his workers to manage a specific amount of resources for him while he's gone. We know the bad guy in this story is the one who was afraid to risk losing what he'd been given, the one who hid his money in the ground and therefore failed to produce any return on his investment. But the other two men involved were faithful in putting their seed money to work and ended up doubling what these two had originally started with.

What, then, was their boss's response when he got back from his trip and saw what they'd been able to achieve? *Well done, guys.* "You were faithful over a few things; I will put you in charge of many things" (vv. 21, 23).

See the progression? From "a few things" to "many things."

Responsibility builds upon itself.

One of the outgrowths of proving responsible in managing yourself and your own business wisely is being given the additional privilege of handling even *more* responsibility. Granted, this comes with its own new set of challenges that will often stretch you beyond your comfort areas. It will bring you out of safe hiding places where you'd perhaps hoped to go unnoticed. But like the landowner in Jesus' parable, who invited his faithful servants to "share your master's joy," the rewards of taking on new responsibilities also come with new, satisfying paybacks all their own.

As a head coach, for example, I was responsible for my whole team, not just for my personal morality and my private adherence to principle. As a result, I got to be part of something much greater than myself: being at the helm of winning football programs that were almost always in the thick of national awareness and title contention. That's not something I could've enjoyed without taking on more and more responsibility as a person, as an employer, and as a leader of young men. But it's something I could've wasted or failed to attain if I hadn't been diligent about following through on what those obligations truly entailed.

That's the next step of responsibility.

For example, you certainly know by now that *faith* is crucially important to me. I've shared how I grappled with that, and how I arrived at the decision to confirm my commitment to it, putting relationship with God above everything else. I truly believe He is the One "from whom all blessings flow."

Now when coaching at a state-sponsored university, I'm sure you're well aware that many people and pressure groups would love to gag your efforts at promoting the importance of God in a young person's life. And many well-meaning people in my position feel adequately afraid to speak up about it. But I felt as though part of my assignment in being a head coach was to train my players in becoming spiritually responsible, which I thought would develop not only their life skills but also their playing skills. It was part of my winning strategy. I expected it to pay off not only in their future but on the scoreboard in the fall.

And here's what you find out when you're bold enough to lay that kind of expectation out there—at least in the South, where the Bible Belt still reaches around most of what people value and believe. Despite what the ACLU wants to denounce as being harmful and offensive, the majority of people who make up the rest of the world *love it.* And they're dying for leaders who will promote Christian values and seek to instill them in their kids.

That's just the truth.

Now don't worry, I covered my tracks with the civil liberties folks. I sent out letters to every one of my players' parents before the season started, declaring what I intended to do and offering them the wide-open chance to opt their son out of any program or activity they felt would go against their wishes. This was strictly voluntary. If they had any hesitations whatsoever, I supplied them with both my home and cell phone numbers, invited them to call me at any time, and assured them that any resistance on their part would not be met with playing-time repercussions for their child on my part.

I meant that.

Yet in more than twelve years of coaching, I only had one parent who called asking to decline. And her son was one of my consistent starters, so it's obvious I didn't penalize him.

But here's what I basically laid out before the parents in my letter. First, we were going to attend church together as a team one Sunday—just once—during the season, after which I would encourage the players' attendance at other times but would definitely not require it of them. And second, I would provide their sons various opportunities to hear faith-based speakers and be part of other motivational programs that contained a Christian emphasis. I didn't attempt to hide what I was doing, and the boys' parents were vocal in their enthusiasm for what I was trying to offer them.

One of the most successful things we did was to institute a system developed by our team chaplain, Tony Eubanks, called Spiritual Two-a-Days. Each player was assigned a spiritual mentor from the community, a Christian man who would commit to meeting with him once a week for some kind of personal Bible study and interaction. Out of the eighty-five guys on my football team, usually seventy-five or more would sign up and follow through on it.

The businessmen, church members, and pastors who served as mentors, of course, *loved* the chance to rub shoulders with their Clemson Tiger ballplayers during the week. But it went deeper than that, I believe. The players, for the most part, saw the value in it too—and responded by maintaining a firm commitment both to our team and to their responsibilities as student athletes.

I'll always believe our Two-a-Day program, in conjunction with the other opportunities we made available to help develop their spiritual core, contributed to the low incidences of troublemaking I experienced from my players during my tenure as coach. I think it helped them make better decisions. It turned up the volume on their conscience a little bit, especially on Friday and Saturday nights when they were forced to answer the "should I or shouldn't I" questions rattling around in their heads. My guys ended up doing a lot more "shoulds" than "shouldn'ts" in the years I was there, and it helped keep their names mostly out of the newspapers except for what happened between the hash marks.

I also sought to instill a spiritual element with the coaches on my staff. Each week on Monday mornings at 6:30, Tony led a voluntary Bible study that a number of the coaches and other support staff chose to attend. Then *every* morning during our mandatory staff meeting at 7:00, either one of the other guys or I would be responsible for giving a three-to-five-minute talk on some topic that was positive and encouraging, something that taught a life lesson. Many of these talks did migrate toward Christian themes—more like what you'd call a *devotional*—but I didn't require that they be biblically based. The person who spoke often closed with a prayer, but he certainly didn't have to. I wasn't trying to force anything. But every morning the twenty or so people gathered in my office usually received some kind of spiritual foundation for making their decisions and framing up their day. It was important to me that they understood where their leader was coming from, and I hoped they'd see the value of what Christian faith can bring to every conceivable situation in life.

I'm not saying we can only deal with other Christians as we go about the day-to-day management of our lives, that everyone else should be treated as suspect. But I know when I went looking for an architect and builder to work on our new home recently, I prayed that God would lead me to people who understood us and could relate to our goals. When I sought out a wealth manager to give me counsel on planning and investments, I asked God for wisdom in choosing a person who was guided by principle, not just economic savvy.

If I was in the business world, I'd love to know that the people handling my finances, or making my sales decisions, or traveling out on the road for me were not just skilled at their work but were motivated by high standards. I'd have a much stronger feeling about my people if I knew they were influenced by a personal calling and mission, if I knew the various judgment calls coming across their desk on a given day were being handled by someone with not just a good business head but a sound spiritual life. I'm aware this approach might be controversial, but I'd want to see to it that they were involved in some sort of ongoing program that was reinforcing their character and their understanding of bedrock truths—the kind the Bible teaches and talks about.

Sound too hard to implement? Would it reveal more of your personal agenda than you'd really want exposed? Would it set you up for criticism? Make you feel too accountable for representing Christ in other ways, such as watching your language or controlling your temper?

If you've been given responsibility over a group of people at work, or students in the classroom, or a ministry in your church, or any other setting where you've assumed a position of authority, do whatever you can to invest in the spiritual growth of those under your watch, within whatever limits you're required to maintain.

That's an investment that will benefit everybody.

Tough Calls

Commitment is a character trait that takes time and effort. *Accountability* is a character trait that requires humility and honesty. But *responsibility*, though in one respect a reward for building a consistent level of performance, is certainly no cakewalk either.

Responsible Christian leadership is not the same as being nice.

One thing I knew: I was responsible for my team. And occasionally that meant taking bold, unpopular stands for what I felt was best for the entire program, what I believed was essential to keep us winning and successful.

I've had to fire coaches, for example—not because of rules violations or moral failures, but based on a much more subjective scale of evidence: simple job performance. That's not always a measurement that's easy to describe and delineate, and it's never any fun to challenge it to a man's face. But responsibility sometimes calls for it, and you have to be the one to execute it.

In college coaching, these conversations and decisions almost always occur during Christmastime, soon after the season is over—hardly the time of year when a guy wants to sit his family down and tell them he's out of work, that they'll most likely be looking at relocating (again), perhaps just when everybody had finally gotten settled in school and church and the neighborhood and everything.

It's a tough profession.

Responsibility can bite and be painful.

But no decision of my coaching career was perhaps more visible and explosive than the one involving an athlete on Clemson's 2005–2007 teams, whose very unique family situation created a dynamic that was both inspirational and insubordinate. In the end I was perhaps the only person in an authoritative role at the school who believed 100 percent with the decision I made. But I felt like I possessed the best view of the situation, and I was certain—as potentially damaging as it was from a PR perspective—that I was simply carrying out what *responsibility* is often tasked with doing.

Ray Ray McElrathbey was a talented player from Atlanta with a tragic backstory. His mother had become incapacitated after many years of extreme drug addiction, and his father was equally incapable of providing support for the family due to his gambling troubles and other problems. As a result, the courts had taken the unusual stance of awarding Ray Ray custody of his eleven-year-old brother, Fahmarr.

The uncustomary ruling soon made Ray Ray a darling of the national media, who saw in him a courageous story of a young nineteen-year-old African-American, juggling Division 1-A football, college coursework, and a single parenting role, all in a highly selfless, sacrificial attempt to provide for his kid brother.

True up to a point.

While Ray Ray was appearing on high-profile outlets like *The Oprah Winfrey Show*, being named "Person of the Week" by ABC News, receiving excellence awards from organizations like ESPN and the Orange Bowl, he was also making a habit of disappearing late at night with his friends, leaving Fahmarr with whichever coach had agreed to watch him for the evening.

After injuring his knee and missing most of the 2006 season, he became spotty about showing up for treatment and was also neglecting the academic regulations and guidelines we had set for the team. Players were constantly complaining to me about how he was abusing the privileges that came with his unusual situation, how there was one set of rules for Ray Ray and another set for everybody else. He was pushing the boundaries and demanding special treatment. He was becoming a distraction. And for those reasons alone—not his custody problem, not his race, not any of the things I was roundly accused of—I made the unpopular decision to remove him from athletic participation with the team. He was still allowed to remain on full financial scholarship, which would enable him to graduate if he chose to continue his studies. That much was up to him. I was dismissing him from the team but not abandoning him to fend for himself. And I honestly hoped it would help him. He obviously had a lot to take care of without bearing the added distraction of football.

I remember the AD coming to me and saying: "You're going to do *what?* Everybody loves this guy. Everybody knows what he's up against." The school president wanted to know what in the world I was thinking. The board of trustees was committed to looking into the matter in depth. But I told them all, "Listen, I believe what the young man is trying to do is commendable. And I don't claim to have a good solution to fix the unfortunate problems in his family. But as the coach, I deal with my team every day. That is my main responsibility. And I'm telling you, his presence in and out of the locker room is causing difficulties that threaten the unity of our team and ultimately my ability to put a winner on the field."

Still, this was not received with glowing praise. Nor did I expect it to be. It was a tough situation, and I felt for the young man on many levels. I honestly wasn't just trying to wash my hands of him.

But I had not made my decision lightly or irrationally. I had prayed long and hard about it and had sought good counsel from people whose wisdom I trusted. Bottom line, Ray Ray was not capable of raising a child singlehandedly at that age, not with that many outside responsibilities. And while I was willing to help in supporting him in whatever way I could, it did not seem to be either in his best interests or ours to continue dressing him out on our football team.

It was a hard call, but I felt a *responsible* one.

Sometimes you have to stand all alone. Take the heat and turn the other cheek. Responsibility may feel nice and empowering when you're being wooed for a promotion, or getting a raise, or signing a new contract. But if you're doing your job, responsibility will always come with challenges— the kind where exercising your authority will be met with widespread criticism and misunderstanding. Comes with the territory. Stops at your desk and your office door. And the way you weather those kinds of situations will tell you a lot about what kind of winner you have in you.

Where You're Most Needed

Jesus' third and final story in Matthew 25 is probably the most familiar of all—the judgment day setting where the Son of Man is seen separating the sheep from the goats, inviting the faithful to receive "the kingdom prepared for you from the foundation of the world . . ."

> For I was hungry and you gave Me something to eat; I was thirsty and you gave Me something

to drink; I was a stranger and you took Me in; I
was naked and you clothed Me; I was sick and
you took care of Me; I was in prison and you
visited Me. (vv. 35–36)

In Jesus' story the ones to whom He's speaking cannot
recall ever seeing Him in any of these pitiful conditions—
starving, abandoned, unclothed, anemic. They certainly don't
understand, then, how they can be rewarded for ministering
to Him in a time of need like that. But He opens their minds
to see that "whatever you did for one of the least of these
brothers of Mine, you did for Me" (v. 40). Every act of service
performed in Jesus' name is like serving Him directly. It's an
offering of grateful worship.

As Christians, as leaders, as people who have been blessed
with resources that can be used to bring comfort and relief
to others, we are not just *encouraged* to give whatever we can
spare to ease the pain of those in need. We are actually *responsible* to care for others out of the plenty that we've received
from God's hand.

Obviously, this follows a recurring theme that runs from
one end of the Bible to the other. God instructed the ancient
Hebrews in the Old Testament to make special provision for
the outcast and disenfranchised. "Happy is the one who cares
for the poor," David wrote in the Psalms, "the LORD will save
him in a day of adversity" (41:1). In one of the most succinct

summary statements in all the Bible, James (most likely the brother of Jesus) says, "Pure and undefiled religion before our God and Father is this: to look after orphans and widows in their distress and to keep oneself unstained by the world" (James 1:27).

And while a whole other book could be written concerning our responsibility to model Christ's compassion by reaching out to the needy, I feel compelled to close this chapter by reiterating a responsibility I addressed in the last one. Sometimes it's easier (in some ways) to get involved in a cause, carrying out heroic acts of mercy and concern for the hurting, than to perform the often much more unheralded duty of meeting your own children's spiritual needs. Because even though your kids may not be hungry or thirsty or naked or in prison, they are still "in need" of a father's concentrated care and counsel. Children at home are still "weak" in comparison to grown, mature adults and are navigating a culture that far outweighs them in terms of pressures, temptations, and enticements to conform.

It is not our responsibility to save our children. Only God can do that. But His desire is to use us as parents (and again, especially as fathers) to *teach* them, *direct* them, and *guide* them toward making wise decisions, including the most important decision of all—receiving forgiveness of their sins through faith in Jesus Christ.

God has also put us in this role of parenting to *protect* our children, to ask questions like: "Where are you going tonight? Who's driving? Whose house are you going to? Will the parents be there? Who else is going with you? What are you going to do after that?" We are responsible to put guard-rails around their lives, to aim them toward friends and other families who will support the standards we're attempting to grow in them, knowing that "bad company corrupts good morals" (1 Cor. 15:33).

We're also here to *pray* for them continually, asking God to keep them within the boundaries of His will, especially when they're making decisions that can affect the whole course of their lives. Every day for twenty-three years I prayed that my daughter would marry a godly man, and every day for twenty-six years I prayed that my son would marry a godly woman . . . until the Lord answered all those hun-dreds of prayers with the exact husband and wife He desired for each one of them. Fathers are charged with going to the mat—literally!—going to their knees in seeking God's favor for their children. It is part of our larger responsibility.

We are responsible for ourselves as individuals.

We are responsible for those we've been assigned to lead.

We are responsible to serve people who are weak and helpless.

And we are responsible to be spiritually engaged with our families.

You can do a lot of things in life. Some good, some bad. But you will only prime yourself for being successful if you take deliberate, determined ownership of the responsibilities you've been given by God to manage. The power behind people who live purposeful, meaningful lives is fueled by the difference *responsibility* makes.

8

Discipline

I was a *loud* coach. I admit it.

Being responsible for the performance and effort of my team meant that I was often on their backs, up in their face masks, riding them hard and at high volume. I may seem a little more low-key and laid-back now, but I assure you, it's just barely disguising a side of my personality that comes out screaming at football season.

Part of my style can probably be attributed to the fact that I spent a good portion of my career as a position coach responsible for wide receivers. The simple physics of communicating with a player who's fifty-three yards across the field, much closer to the opposite sideline than he is to yours, requires a strong set of pipes if you want to feed him any instructions (or to chew him out, whichever objective applies at the moment).

But I certainly can't blame *all* my coaching tendencies on that. I was just hands-on by nature. I'd grab guys by the shoulder pads and jerk them into position. I'd pop them hard on the helmet if I didn't think I was getting through to their thick heads. I never used profanity. I can promise you that. But I'm not saying I was always flattering either. I expected a certain level of intensity from my players, and the sooner they understood and responded in kind, the less they were forced to put up with my yelling.

One of the guys who coached on my staff, both at Tulane and at Clemson, was Rich Rodriguez, formerly of West Virginia and Michigan, currently head coach at the University of Arizona. Rich was my offensive coordinator for several years, and sometimes when we felt the players were underperforming or needed a good shake-down, we'd team up to rattle their cages a little bit.

When you go into the dressing room at halftime of a game, the coaches usually meet first by themselves to assess what they've seen so far and to discuss the adjustments and corrections they want to make in the second half. Only after that do you typically meet with your players to give them instructions for the remainder of the game. But sometimes *instruction* is not what they need the most. They need *incentive*.

Maybe *in stereo*.

So every now and then, I'd say to Rich before we went in to talk to the players, "Hey, let's do the old good-cop, bad-cop." Either he'd do the stroking and I'd do the yelling or the other way around—I'd do the stroking and *he'd* do the yelling. Whichever way, we made sure our team got the clear message that their energy and hustle were lacking, that we were challenging their toughness. We were calling out their best effort. Asking for more.

No, *demanding* more.

Now football, I know, is football—much like the army is the army. The same scare tactics a leader might employ to inject emotion into his team probably wouldn't apply to most other situations in life. Hollering and hitting people—the way a coach sometimes does to get his players' attention—would be highly inappropriate anywhere else besides the sideline or the locker room.

(I wish my mother had known that.)

But even when it's not being delivered to you with loud rants and whistles and thrown clipboards, the expectation of *discipline* remains a key component of a winning character. Any football team that doesn't excel in being focused, attentive, poised, and under control will trip up somewhere before they reach that fine line—the one that exists between victory and failure—the one that nobody wants standing between themselves and the places they're trying to reach in life.

Who Do You Want to Be Like?

When you think of *discipline,* especially in spiritual terms, you may perceive it as being a private matter, something that's confined to your personal times of prayer and Bible reading— or what are commonly called the "spiritual disciplines." Certainly there's a lot to be said, of course, for getting alone with God, ideally on a daily basis, long enough to enjoy some uninterrupted moments of worship, listening, and meditation on His Word.

But discipline, in its most powerful form, is not gained entirely through being alone. Isolation is not the goal. Striving to be disciplined is not merely an attempt to achieve some kind of grit-your-teeth mastery over your mind and body.

In fact, the Bible doesn't actually teach us to *isolate* ourselves at all. It talks instead about *separating* ourselves, which is something else altogether. Being isolated makes you odd. You repel people. You push others away. You turn your pursuit of inner strength into a solo sport that no one else is really a part of or understands.

Being "separate," on the other hand (2 Cor. 6:17), simply means you're different. A *different* kind of person. You stand out. There's something special about you. A recognizable goodness and character. In a world of people who all seem to be doing the same things, chasing the same ambitions, hanging out at the same places, and defining fun the same way, you're remarkably distinctive. You're unique. Uncommon.

Not everyone knows what to call that when they see it. They may not be able to put their finger on why you seem to appeal to them or inspire them. But it goes by the name of *discipline*. It's the way people look when they're not all talk. It's how people live when they're serious about improving themselves—physically, mentally, spiritually. It's what people do when they're hot on the trail of excellence instead of just running with the pack off a cliff of mediocrity.

Discipline doesn't make people want to *avoid* you. Instead, it *attracts* people to you—because when you're truly disciplined, it's not *strangeness* that shows but rather your *strength*.

And the way you hone that strength is not by closeting yourself off, becoming oddly introspective, but by seeking out and being around the people you most want to be like—people who are working hard to develop the same kind of character muscles *you're* trying to grow—people who love God, value His Word, and are trying their best to bring their lives into alignment with it.

So if you don't think you've got what it takes to be disciplined, if you're not the type who likes being by yourself or sitting still for long periods of time, that's all right. Because that's not all there is to it. Discipline is most effectively hammered out in conjunction with other people—as long as the people you're getting around are making you better instead of worse, calling you higher instead of lower, challenging you to be stronger instead of coddling your weaknesses, digging up character you didn't know was inside you.

The way a loud coach does.

If I wanted my teams to be tough, I didn't have any other choice. Football is a game of toughness. It's not a contact sport. (*Basketball* is a contact sport.) Football is a *collision* sport. In order to have my guys ready for the brute force of big-college football, I needed tough players, built up by tough workout regimens, pushed by the steady friction of tough practices, trained hard by tough coaches.

Nothing less puts a winner on the field.

And nothing less will do it for you either.

There's a reason fish swim in schools. Birds fly in a flock. Cows travel in a herd. Insects join up in colonies. God embeds in His creatures a need for being together and working in groups. And for us human beings—the highest form of God's creation—this need for interaction becomes a cognizant desire. In fact, if you *don't* desire to be with other godly men, or as women with other godly women, you're more or less admitting that you've got something to hide, that you've quit trying to be your best, that you've dipped down to a certain level of acceptable effort that you don't want challenged by anybody else.

You're letting go of *discipline*.

And I urge you—don't do it.

I can yell if I have to.

This is no time to let up. The game's not anywhere close to being over yet. People are counting on you to dig in, not veg out.

And a good place to start is by involving yourself more closely with the friends, couples, and coworkers who can do you the most moral and spiritual good. Together you'll help hold one another accountable for standing tough against temptation and staying tenacious about pursuing God's highest goals for your life, living for Him in the real world yet also *separating* yourself from it at the same time.

Discipline grows best when we're grinding it out against one another.

No Compromise

Some of the most basic, specific advice for anyone wanting to live a disciplined lifestyle is this: *you must not compromise God's Word.*

People find it easy to diminish the importance of the Bible, especially as it relates to having any real bearing on a person's daily decisions and behavior. They say, "Look, the Bible was written more than two thousand years ago. There can't be much of anything in there about the questions people are asking today."

True, the Bible was written long before cell phones, before computers, before hybrid cars, and before McDonald's milk shakes. But everyday items and experiences like these are actually just cultural details. They happen to be the playing pieces that are out on the board at this moment. But if you wait ten years, they'll be replaced by something else, something snazzier, something everybody's got to have. Yet they'll all still be governed by the same principles that apply to every age and every generation.

"Jesus Christ is the same yesterday, today, and forever" (Heb. 13:8). "Heaven and earth will pass away," He said, "but My words will never pass away" (Mark 13:31). That's some plain talk on the subject of how relevant the Bible is. If you ask me, that pretty much answers the question about whether it has anything to say to us right here, right now, at our current street address and GPS location.

The only real question that remains is whether we're going to follow it.

Without compromise.

Daniel was a guy from Bible days who lived a "no compromise" lifestyle. He had been hauled away from his home in Jerusalem by the wicked, imperial regime of King Nebuchadnezzar of Babylon. He was now living in a foreign country where going along with what his captors demanded— the status quo—was both encouraged and expected. Yet he consistently held on to his beliefs and to what those deep convictions required of him.

When told to eat a Babylonian diet, for example, as part of a special program for governmental advancement, he refused to defile himself by partaking of food the Hebrew Scriptures declared unclean.

When presented with the opportunity to use his God-given skills of wisdom and interpretation in return for a handsome payment of gifts and increased status in the kingdom, he performed the service that was being asked of him but said, "You may keep your gifts, and give your rewards to someone else" (Dan. 5:17). That's not what drove or defined him. God did.

When trapped by a bogus law that made it illegal to pray to any other "god" except the king, Daniel went home (like always), faced the window that opened toward Jerusalem (like always), "got down on his knees, prayed, and gave thanks to his God, just as he had done before" (6:10). Like always.

He wasn't about to compromise *anything*—no matter where he was and no matter what people wanted him to do or not do.

And even though that kind of attitude did win him some sworn enemies—as true belief often tends to do—his decision to heed God's standards and principles did not ultimately keep him from earning the respect of those who were holding him against his will. He still rose to the highest echelons of power and authority in Babylon despite staying true to his core precepts. He found a way to work within a pagan system without wavering on what was central to his spiritual foundation.

Sounds like a good guy for us to be around and to learn from.

Be looking for people like that.

The prophet Jeremiah is another one—a true example of uncompromising character. He was a young man who had no desire to be a spokesman for God among his native people. But when the Lord basically gave him no other choice, telling him, "Do not be afraid of anyone, for I will be with you to deliver you" (Jer. 1:8), he obediently went out and proclaimed God's message.

More often than not, the speeches God told him to give were ones of challenge, warning, and judgment to the people of Judah. Hard words. Confrontational. Not easy at all to say. Jeremiah wasn't by nature the provocative type. He took no pleasure in pointing out others' failures (like some people seem to do). Yet he stood tall anyway and spoke what God had told him to speak.

Without compromise.

Oh, he would get frustrated sometimes. The people wouldn't listen. They weren't willing to look in the mirror and see the plain-as-day reality that what he was saying about them was the absolute truth. Eventually they would make him pay for his irritating boldness by convicting him of treason and throwing him in jail. When that didn't slow him down, they tossed him into a dank, muddy cistern and left him there, hoping he'd die. History would be correct in remembering him as the "weeping prophet."

But God would continue to say to him, "Stand in the courtyard of the LORD's temple and speak all the words I have commanded you to speak to all Judah's cities that are coming to worship there. *Do not hold back a word*" (26:2). And even though it cost him nearly everything he had in terms of reputation, security, companionship, and peace of mind—even though in his dark moments he would acknowledge that "the word of the LORD has become for me constant disgrace and derision"—he would still be compelled to come right back and admit, *Yeah, but,* "If I say, 'I won't mention Him or speak any longer in His name,' His message becomes a fire burning in my heart, shut up in my bones" (20:8–9).

When it was all said and done for Jeremiah—no compromise.

And when you're looking for heroes, look for people like that.

They'll lead you toward sound *discipline.*

The Bible doesn't change, any more than its Author does. That's why those of us who resolve to live a disciplined life as His followers cannot vacillate when it comes to carrying out His commands. Whatever else we do, we cannot go soft on His Word. If that's not what's driving us, we will come out flat and look sloppy on most days. We'll end up playing without heart and emotion. We'll waste all of that hard work and effort we put into life and end up spending far too much of it on a losing cause.

Nobody wants that.

Getting Everyone's Best

It goes without saying, I think, that God holds us to a high standard. Jesus said it this way: "Be perfect, therefore, as your heavenly Father is perfect" (Matt. 5:48).

Now obviously, we're not capable of living without any fault or blame whatsoever. Nobody can be "perfect." But the standard He keeps before us is still way up there. The mark doesn't move. You don't become a winner by settling for less but by trusting Christ to transform you continually into someone who actually lives the way a Christian is supposed to live. And you *really can do it*—not on your own, of course, but because "it is God who is working in you, enabling you both to will and to act for His good purpose" (Phil. 3:13).

Like Paul said about himself:

> I have been crucified with Christ; and I no lon-
> ger live, but Christ lives in me. The life I now
> live in the body, I live by faith in the Son of
> God, who loved me and gave Himself for me.
> (Gal. 2:19–20)

We are saved in order to be serious about Him, to let Him continually change us through daily, hard-fought, hard-won discipline.

But just as the call to discipline means expecting a lot of ourselves, it also means expecting a lot of others. You cannot afford to hold back the brutal honesty that's sometimes needed if you want to help another person, child, or work group perform up to speed, even if it means being tougher on them than you might actually want to be.

Every August I'd kick off the official start of the football year by convening a comprehensive get-together with all the people on my staff—coaching staff, weight staff, video staff, training staff, academic staff, everybody. We'd go over my entire plan of operation, how I proposed to address things from a coaching perspective throughout the season. And one of the topics I always included as part of that meeting was a discussion of the recruiting rules and my plan for dealing with any coach who didn't follow the guidelines—no matter how important his job was or how close we were as friends and work associates.

Now like I've said before, the laundry list of NCAA recruiting stipulations could be murky and subject to misunderstanding. The particulars were constantly being tweaked to prevent any school or program from gaining a competitive advantage over another. But each year every coach at every member school was required to take a test sanctioned by the NCAA that spelled out the current rules and noted any changes from previous seasons. So as complicated as the codebook could be, we all had to admit that we'd at least been presented with the overall parameters.

So I came right out and told them at that meeting, "Guys, everybody knows the rules. If you get caught breaking them, I *will* not back you. You *will* be gone."

In other words, they'd better exercise some discipline if they knew what was good for them.

Over the course of my career, I did have to reprimand a few of my coaches for stepping over the line regarding some of the *secondary* violations—being a little too aggressive, making a few too many phone calls, spending a minute or two longer with a recruit than they should, like if they happened to bump into him inadvertently in the hallway at his high school. But I never had to deal with any major rules infractions that I recall by any members of my staff, and I think it's largely because we'd already crossed that bridge from the get-go. I had presented my terms to them in the most black-and-white way I could.

Compromise *would not* be tolerated. They knew it.

Only solid self-discipline would be accepted.

I'm not sure, of course, how this approach translates specifically to your own life. But if you have a family, for example, it might mean explaining to your children the rules of the house and letting them know precisely what will happen if they choose to sidestep them. If you supervise a handful of people at work, it means you don't let an employee's lack of effort slide just because you're afraid of having an awkward conversation with him.

Pick your personal situation, and paste this principle inside of it. After all, you're not doing people any favors by failing to inspire them to peak performance, both by your own example of excellence and by being clear and to the point with the instructions you give them.

That's just the way it's got to be. You call people *up* to discipline. You set the standard high. Yes, you treat them fair, and you do it with class and respect. But you also let them know that they are required to tend to their business at a certain level of efficiency. Only then will they be able to succeed personally while also contributing to the success of the whole.

No, you don't have to be a drill sergeant about it. You can do it with a humble, Christ-like spirit. As they say, meekness is not the same as weakness. In fact, I've heard *meekness* defined as being "controlled power." It's sort of like what Carl Sandburg wrote of Abraham Lincoln when he described him as being "steel and velvet." More importantly, it's what Jesus Christ was like when He walked the earth—a tough-minded Man who was not afraid to challenge His guys to devotion and discipline. You should never equate His leadership style with weakness and tolerance.

People will tend to sink to the lowest rung of expectations you place on them. They'll rarely rise up on their own initiative unless you lay the challenge out there for them, showing them what to strive for . . . and what failure to work for it will cost. So be willing to step on some toes if that's what necessary to lead people from half measures to full success. Dare them to be their very best.

They'll thank you for it one day . . . when it draws out the real winner in them.

Highs and Lows

Ask any coach, no matter what sport you're talking about, and he'll tell you that every season is a daily, weekly, sometimes hourly process of responding to both winning and losing, to moments of success and moments of failure. You certainly hope to win more than you lose, of course, but you obviously can't win every game, every time, every year. So how does your team respond after a close loss? A close win? A blowout by the other team? A runaway victory against a substandard opponent?

Your season will largely rise and fall based on the character of these various responses.

How do you respond, for example, when you come out strong from the opening play of the game and build a big early lead? Do you keep your intensity level up the rest of the way, or do you eventually start coasting instead?

How do you respond to being ahead by ten points as you're entering the fourth quarter? What about when you're ten points behind? What about when you're so far behind in the last five minutes, there's no possible way you can catch up and win the game? Do you pack it in and quit, start thinking about your date tonight, or do you keep pushing yourself to excel?

Winning. Losing. Responding.

It all takes discipline.

Every game, every season follows this rhythm of highs and lows. That's why one of the main jobs for a head coach is learning how to motivate his team and his staff throughout any kind of winning or losing scenario. You cannot let a loss beat you twice by allowing discouragement to hang around till the next game. Neither can you let a winning streak tempt your players into believing everything that's being written about them in the newspapers. They cannot be glued to their highlight package when they need to be breaking down tape of their upcoming opponent.

The Bible paints for us a lot of different winning and losing situations and teaches us how a person of character is supposed to handle them. The Old Testament book of Deuteronomy, for example—a name that means "second law"—is basically a refresher course on the standards and expectations of the covenant that God laid out with Moses before sending Him down Mount Sinai with the Ten Commandments. The ancient Israelites at this time, although continuing to experience some difficulties and challenges, were in the midst of a thrilling string of victories their people had not seen in more than four hundred years. It was exciting. Exhilarating. But when winning is starting to feel easy, as though somebody owes it to you, that's a good time for a reminder. And that's why over and over again throughout the book of Deuteronomy, you hear this familiar phrase: "Don't forget."

God urged His people to remember everything He had done to spring them free from Egyptian slavery, how He had pummeled their captors with plagues of hail and frogs and gnats and so forth, ultimately killing all the firstborn sons throughout the entire country to get mighty Pharaoh finally to relent and let them go.

Don't forget.

Remember too, He said, the many ways He had protected them on their journey forward—like parting the Red Sea to keep the Egyptian armies from overtaking them, like miraculously spewing fresh water out of dry rock, like sending manna to cover the ground each morning, meeting their physical needs in supernatural ways.

Don't forget.

He also reminded them how the whole point of their deliverance was to lead them to the promised land, where they would represent the name of God among enemy nations, and where they and their children would enjoy the blessings of plenty and prosperity.

But . . .

> When you eat and are full, and build beautiful houses to live in, and your herds and your flocks grow large, and your silver and gold multiply, and everything else you have increases, be careful that your heart doesn't become proud and you forget the LORD your God who brought you out of the land of Egypt, out of the place of slavery. (Deut. 8:12–14)

Don't forget.

You cannot rest on your laurels while the game is still going on. You cannot afford to lose awareness of what it's like to lose, to be hungry, to scrape by, to want victory so bad you can taste it. Above all, you cannot let yourself believe for one minute that you're the one who's ultimately responsible for your success, as if you could do it without God's help—the One who can take away your success overnight if you get stars in your eyes and don't keep your feet on the ground.

Don't forget. Stay disciplined.

Perhaps you're experiencing a time of success and glory in your life right now. Things are going pretty well for you. Good money. Comfortable lifestyle. You're the envy of your old friends. Understand, though, that victory is not meant to be a destination but more like a thrusting mechanism spurring you toward the next challenge. Don't ever become so enamored with your achievements that you forget what it took to get you there.

That makes me think of another Old Testament example. King David, who was beginning to experience some real success as Israel's ruler, felt he had earned permission to stay home one spring when most kings traditionally marched out for war. As a result—you know the story—the opportunity presented itself for him to give in to lustful desire, and he committed a passionate act of adultery with Bathsheba. He then followed that up by planning a heartless crime of murder when he arranged for her husband to be "accidentally" killed in battle.

David had gone from a long run of heralded victories to a sudden, humiliating defeat—a scenario most all of us know pretty well, in one form or another. Number one in the country had just been dealt a stunning upset loss. How would he respond? What would he do?

Obviously his defeat would leave lasting repercussions. No amount of redemption would ever remove the effects of those sins from his life and from his family, any more than you can go back and change the won-lost records of past seasons to match what you wish had happened. But the depth of David's repentance, expressed so painfully and raw in his words from Psalm 51, tells the story of a man who was willing to pick apart every reason behind his failure. To learn what had caused it. No excuses. Whatever he was suffering personally—guilt, regret, remorse, sadness, bitter anger with himself—wasn't really the worst of it, and he knew it. He'd not only let himself down; he'd let God down. "Against You— You alone—I have sinned and done this evil in Your sight. So You are right when You pass sentence; You are blameless when You judge" (v. 4).

And yet out of that pit of ugly defeat—down where David could have been tempted to quit, down where he could have decided not to deal head-on with responsibility—he made the choice all winners must ultimately make after a crushing loss. He was coming back. He was taking his medicine. It wasn't going to be easy. He was braced for the extra effort required of his recovery. But he believed God would give him the tools to be victorious again, even stronger than before.

> Purify me with hyssop, and I will be clean; wash me, and I will be whiter than snow. . . . God, create a clean heart for me and renew a steadfast spirit within me. Do not banish me from Your presence or take your Holy Spirit from me.

Restore the joy of your salvation to me, and give
me a willing spirit. (vv. 7, 10–12)

Maybe, instead of coming off a string of back-to-back victories, you're more like David right now, dealing with a deep
personal loss, perhaps even bogged down in a long losing skid.
You're tripping over the same sins that have been dogging you
for years. You're smarting from financial mistakes that have
put you behind the eight ball, just as the sluggish economy
was closing off the most customary ways of bouncing back.
You've allowed your marriage and family relationships to sour
into bitterness and distance. You're beat down from trying
hard and coming up short, time after time.

Then listen to this loud old football coach telling you
what you probably need to hear. Quit feeling sorry for yourself. Learn from your mistakes. Get your head back in the
game. Now is not the time to deflate or despair. It's time to
get up and get back to work. Costly work. Committed work.
Accountable work. Responsible work.

Sweat. Blood. Trust. Teamwork.

Or maybe you'd recognize it by its other name.

Discipline.

9

Sacrifice

S acrifice" is one of the Bible's most common themes. Just
about every one of its sixty-six books mentions the idea
in some fashion or another, occasionally in gruesome detail.

Genesis, of course, includes the account of Abraham
being told to offer his only son, Isaac, as a sacrifice—the
ultimate test of a man's willingness to trust God's promises.
Much of Exodus, as well as parts of Leviticus, Numbers, and
Deuteronomy, spell out the ceremonial requirements of the
Old Testament law, which (among other things) included
the various kinds of sacrifices that corresponded with certain
feast days, worship observances, and other matters of ancient
religious lifestyle.

Going on from there, as you read through the books
that follow, you come across numerous examples of people

bringing sacrifices to God, typically overseen by priests at the Hebrew tabernacle. Later, when the first temple was finally dedicated during the reign of King Solomon, the long parade of sacrifices was so massive—twenty-two thousand cattle and 120,000 sheep, not to mention the grain offerings and other worship gifts—the whole thing had to be moved out into the temple courtyard. The main altar wasn't large enough to accommodate it all.

All that sacrifice.

It's hard for us to understand. To our modern ears and tastes, it just seems like a lot of needless killing and slaughtering. But here and there, even in the Old Testament, a few people began to get the message that God was not actually bloodthirsty for animal flesh. What He truly wanted was His people's hearts, not their livestock.

Samuel, for instance, understood that "to obey is better than sacrifice" (1 Sam. 15:22)—similar to what David said: "The sacrifice pleasing to God is a broken spirit . . . a broken and humbled heart" (Ps. 51:17). These men realized the Lord was no fool. He wasn't looking to be appeased by ceremonies, by religious rites followed down to the letter. The sacrificial system was merely a vehicle for expressing the sense of worship and dependence on God that hopefully came from somewhere deep inside—the only place where genuine sacrifice can truly begin.

But more than anything, *sacrifice* painted a living (and dying) picture of a universal truth—that "without the shedding of blood there is no forgiveness" (Heb. 9:22). Human sin can never be penalty free. Someone has to pay. Not with twenty dollars out of his pocket or with a promise to do better but with his own life's blood.

And if not for a substitute, that blood would eventually have to be ours.

But that wasn't God's desire. So in the spiritual economy of the Old Testament, He allowed for helpless animals to bear the guilt of human sin. Seeing them butchered before their owners' eyes was meant to communicate in a most visible way two important things: (1) the grave seriousness of failing to meet God's standards, and (2) the reality of His grace.

Sacrifice, in other words, is what kept sinful men in the game. It left open the pathway to life and victory and paved the way for Someone else to offer the most perfect sacrifice of all—the sacrifice that led to our ultimate victory—when Jesus, the spotless Lamb without blemish, "entered the most holy place once for all, not by the blood of goats and calves, but by His own blood" in order to "cleanse our consciences from dead works to serve the living God" (Heb. 9:12, 14).

Through Christ's sacrifice, we are given our one and only opportunity to be saved from sin. His death shows us in bloody, painful, gut-wrenching detail just how important— eternally important—this matter of *sacrifice* really is.

So when viewed in comparison with the cross, we hope-fully realize that no sacrifice of ours is too great to give back to Him. When He says, "If anyone wants to come with Me, he must deny himself, take up his cross daily, and follow Me" (Luke 9:23), we should know He's not asking something of us He wasn't willing to do Himself.

But because He has paid the supreme sacrifice—the one intended to "free those who were held in slavery all their lives by the fear of death" (Heb. 2:15)—*we* are now free to experience the ongoing victories that sacrifice alone is able to win, even when performed on the much smaller, much more personal scale we call our everyday lives.

Christ has shown us what real sacrifice is. And what it can do.

It's up to us now to give Him opportunities to keep proving it.

Time to Sacrifice

When my staff got together for that first big meeting of the season every year—the one I talked about in the last chapter—I always took the occasion to remind them of several things. And one of them was that the cost of winning football games would include a greater outlay of their time than most "normal" people are required to invest in their careers. It's just the nature of our profession.

During the stretch of months between that August meeting and the national signing day in February, they'd be watching a whole lot of football but probably not a whole lot of their kid's basketball games, their volleyball games, their soccer games, their gymnastic events, their ballet and violin recitals, or anything else that required them to knock off early or be free on a Friday night. There simply would not be enough hours in the day or enough time left over at the end of the week to be a regular at many of their children's activities.

"But remember, guys, y'all have chosen this," I said to them. They had made the decision to be football coaches on the college level. They knew the kind of hours that I (or any other head coach) would demand of them . . . and of myself. But I felt like it was important to restate this reality for them, mainly so they would be sure to sit down with their wives and families before the season got any further along, just to clarify expectations from the outset.

Some of these men had been coaching for years. They'd been down this trail before. But in case their time-consuming jobs were a cause of ongoing friction at home, I just wanted to encourage them to be responsible for communicating to their families in such a way that nobody would be caught blindsided by their husband's and dad's work responsibilities.

Now obviously I'm not saying the first place you can start looking to cut and make sacrifices is by neglecting your family. In fact, I promised my staff at that meeting—and I meant it—that I would give them time off in the spring, and even more in the summer, to make up for the time they'd missed during the heart of the football season. But I challenged them that when those lighter months did roll around, they needed to make the absolute most of them. Don't be putting your wife and kids last when you finally do get the luxury of being together more.

For now, though, everybody was going to be required to make some sacrifices.

The sacrifice of *time*.

Any great accomplishment involves the willingness to invest more time into a task than you might really want to give. And in order to deposit your time into that account, it'll need to be withdrawn from somewhere else. Twenty-four hours a day is a zero-sum game. You can't make more. You can only move it from one place to another.

Perhaps all you're being asked to give up are things you don't have any business doing anyway—the various wastes of time and compromises of character that have steered you away from responsibility and maximum achievement before. Or perhaps you're being asked to set aside activities during this particular season of life that would normally be OK for you to do—watching television, going hunting, managing your fantasy baseball team, sleeping late on Saturdays. But to do what the important job in front of you requires, these fun and games cannot be tolerated at the moment. Nothing so trivial and self-serving can be allowed to distract your passion and focus. That stuff will have to be saved for later.

Or maybe—like the guys on my coaching staff—the temporary cost of achievement in your life is something that hurts you every time you think about it. You're having to miss special times with your family. You're forced to pass up offers of extra, paying work, wondering if the same chances, clients, and customers will be there again when you're free enough to get back to them. Or perhaps you're needing to curtail your involvement in a volunteer service opportunity that you're genuinely drawn toward—and which some people can make you feel guilty for declining—even when that's the wisest choice for you to make . . . for now.

But sacrifice is often the price of improvement and success. The expenditure of dedicated *time*, uninterrupted *time*, preciously guarded *time* is one of the keys that can unlock that feeling you get (though so few ever get it) of actually approaching your full potential.

How many times have you decided *your time* is not worth sacrificing for that?

At Critical Points

Here's another one. Another sacrifice. Most of us have a certain level of people-pleasing in us. And while there's definitely a healthy aspect to such an inborn trait—(nobody, for example, should want to be as unlikable as possible)—let's not deny that a lot of pride, fear, and insecurity is wrapped up inside it. Too often we *need* others to be impressed by us. If they're not—if they show us disapproval or they dismiss us as unimportant—we immediately wear it on our faces and in our attitudes. We drive home defeated by it, trying to figure out what we did wrong. We get angry and touchy. Confused and depressed. And as a result, we find out real quickly just how wedded we are to our own reputation.

But if you spend a lot of time obsessing about whether or not people are noticing you, congratulating you, or thinking highly enough of you, you'll lose sight of what's required to stay sharp under pressure. If you intend to be successful at something, others' criticism will always be part of the bargain. Just go ahead and count on that. Not everyone will like the way you think, the decisions you make, the leadership style you employ, the way you comb your hair or run your meetings, or even how you say hello to them in the morning.

They'll find something not to like. And they'll tell somebody. And eventually, all that talking and telling will get back around to *you*.

I don't know how many times, for example, I'd be filling my coffee cup before Sunday school during football season when a guy would come up behind me, pat me hard on the back, and tell me in the most reassuring manner, "You know, Coach, I don't care what they say about you. I still like you."

Wait—who's saying what? What did they say?

You just have to tune all of that out. You can't be like a hitter up at bat in baseball who's got the proverbial "rabbit ears," who's dialed in to all the jokes and cheap shots coming out of the stands behind him. You just can't take that stuff personally. Can't dwell on it. You can't afford to give negativity a place to attach itself in your mind because it'll quickly put down roots and start displacing all that sense of mission and confidence you've been working so hard and for so long to cultivate there.

You do not have a choice but to sacrifice your addiction to other people's approval and acceptance. Not if you want to win.

College sports is a classic training ground for making this trade-off. Most people don't realize that a head coach is not only responsible for keeping his team of nineteen- and twenty-year-olds energized and ready to play, but also for maintaining the morale of the thirty-, forty-, and fifty-year-olds who man his coaching staff—the ones who are more likely than his players are to be around him in unguarded moments, to feel his doubts and uncertainties rubbing off on them.

The head coach simply cannot let himself walk into a staff meeting with a long face and then expect to inspire the guys who work with him. He cannot wither under the heat of public opinion and still do the job that he and his team have been asked to perform at a championship level. I'm not saying there aren't legitimate questions people ought to be allowed to ask in your presence. The tone of any thriving workplace should invite the kinds of challenges that make everyone better, brighter, more alert, and more adept—including you! But good leaders must learn fast that the acclaim of the masses is not what you hang your hat on any more than you hang your head at their cutting remarks and critiques.

Winning comes from laying down your right to be adored in order to throw down the best effort you've got inside.

"I don't care *what* they say about you."

A Lifestyle of Sacrifice

I signed a lot of guys to play football for me who were a little rough around the edges. Guys who had been in some trouble in high school. Guys who had struggled to keep their grades up. Guys who had shown a lot of talent for shedding blockers but not always for blocking out temptation. Success as a college athlete under my rules and my expectations—for them—was going to be a *sacrifice*.

One thing I really stressed as a coach was academics. Compared year to year with other Clemson football teams from past seasons, ours consistently broke records for the highest overall GPA, the most academic All-Americans, the best graduation rates, and other categories like that. Still couldn't beat Duke head-to-head academically across the conference, and certainly couldn't compete with the grades of our golf and swimming teams at our own school. But for football players who'd never set foot on a golf course before, and couldn't swim a lap in the pool even if their next meal was waiting for them at the other end, I thought we held our own pretty well.

But it didn't come without sacrifice.

I think of one guy in particular—a player I recruited out of Louisiana who came in with grades so poor he was actually reading on a third-grade level. One of his former teachers—whether out of genuine concern or just to make a point, I was never sure—had sent me an e-mail that predicted this young man would *never* be able to earn a college diploma. And I'm sure he *wouldn't* have, if not for sacrificing a huge chunk of his social life, if not for going to the academic learning center when others were going out for the night, if not for spending a lot of time with tutors and learning specialists—the folks who do such hard-nosed, heroic work on college campuses across the country.

This young man hadn't shown up on campus with a lot of training in study skills, time management skills, reading and writing skills. But five years of sheer sacrifice later, he had earned the right to walk across that stage to be awarded his bachelor's degree. He had done it.

One day not long before his graduation ceremony, I asked him to stop by my office, and I pulled out that memo I'd kept on file all those years. Handed it to him. Told him how proud I was of him. Next thing I know, tears formed in his eyes. He broke down and cried, right there in my office, right in front of his football coach.

That's a moment earned by sacrifice.

And college athletes have to earn those every day. When their friends are slogging back home from their last class around 2:00, 3:00, ready to take a nap or toss Frisbee in the side yard, my guys had already been up since 5:30 or 6:00 that morning to do their lifting, then hustled from their morning and early afternoon classes in time to make 2:30 meetings. They'd followed that up by being at practice from 3:30 to 6:00, then over to a mandatory study hall after supper, and finally off to bed to make curfew.

But if you want to succeed, you do that. You give up things. You make sacrifice a lifestyle.

You do your workout even if it means not doing lunch. You back away from sinful pleasures that weaken your testimony and grieve the Holy Spirit. You don't let your stomach decide what you put in your mouth today. You trade the lake this weekend for fixing those two or three things around the house that have been irritating your wife lately. You study your Bible before you study the box scores.

You make sacrifices. Everywhere.

Everywhere you want victory to be.

Hard to Say Good-bye

When sacrifice asks for our *time*, that's a hard choice, but we see how it makes sense. We know we shouldn't resent everything that impinges on the freedom of our nights and weekends.

When sacrifice asks for our *reputation*, that's hard too, but it still makes sense. We know we shouldn't be dependent on hearing good things said about us all the time. We know we need to quit overreacting to criticism.

And when sacrifice asks us to make *lifestyle* choices every day that come at the cost of our own comfort, calendar, and convenience . . . that's also hard but again makes sense.

A fourth category of sacrifice, however, may not make any sense to you at all. In fact, it may even sound uncaring, unloving, and un-Christian. But when you're forced into a corner to make this difficult decision, you'll actually be deciding whether you're going to maintain your forward progress in life or stay mired in defeat and frustration.

Ready for it? Here you go.

Sometimes you need to sacrifice *friends*.

I think of this primarily in terms of the players I coached. Young people are typically more engaged in settings that involve a lot of social activities and weekend interaction— more than older adults normally are. The college campus and the single adult scene throw people together in compromising situations where you sometimes never know what's coming at you next. And if the people you've chosen to be around are the kind who don't keep a good check on their lifestyle, who participate in dangerous practices, and who get upset when you won't join in and be part of the peer pressure, you *will* start looking like them. You *will* take the form of the friends you associate with most often.

Argue all you want, but that's just the truth.

And yet it's not only carousing college kids who could choose a better sort of friends than the ones they're currently running with. Older people, too, can get stuck in the habit of accepting invitations from friends who are regular drains on their moral convictions, friends who keep them stuck at an immaturity level that is spiritually confining and conflicting.

For example, you may routinely go out with another married couple where the husband is a fairly free, social drinker. And after he's popped back a few, he tends to get loud, be flirty, and start misbehaving in some of the ways you guys used to carry on in your younger days. But now it makes your wife uncomfortable. It makes you a little uncomfortable, too, if you're being really honest about it. But he's your friend. You've got a history together. You wouldn't want to offend him by having to tell him, "Hey, we're just not going to be able to go out anymore—not if you're going to act *that* way."

That's a hard thing to do. That's a tough sacrifice to make. But no biblical law says that being Christian "nice" means continuing to socialize with people who won't grow up. Instead, the Bible actually tells us just the opposite.

The writer of the book of Hebrews fussed at his readers for being so "slow to understand," for having to be taught over and over again "the basic principles of God's revelation"—when these people ought to be the ones doing the teaching themselves (Heb. 5:11–12). The apostle Paul, irritated with many in the Corinthian church who were not progressing in some major areas of spiritual growth, said he was sick and tired of not being able to speak with them "as spiritual people but as people of the flesh, as babies in Christ" (1 Cor. 3:1).

And as if that wasn't getting personal enough, Paul then fielded a question concerning a fellow believer in their church who was living an immoral lifestyle and refused to give it up. What do you think Paul's instructions were to the church there? Play nice? Just give him some space and some time to come around? Invite him over to dinner and hope the conservation allows you an opening to bring up the subject?

No. Paul ordered them to remove him from their fellowship—because if they didn't, this man's presence and example would become like "yeast" that "permeates the whole batch of dough" (1 Cor. 5:6). The best thing they could do for *him* was to shock him into seeing what his sinful behavior was costing him. And the best thing for *them* was to live without him until he got the message, knowing that as long as he remained unrepentant, he would always have more of an effect on them than they would on him.

Please don't misunderstand me. I'm not saying to be ugly to people or to give yourself permission to feel superior. The Bible is clear that we're supposed to be engaged in the world, involved with all kinds of people—Christians and non-Christians alike. We're not supposed to run off and isolate ourselves. We can't be "salt and light" in the world if we keep it all cooped up inside some kind of religious closet.

But you *will* become like the company you keep—perhaps not like your passing acquaintances but definitely like the people you spend the bulk of your time around, the friends whose opinions really matter most to you.

That's because you *are* what you repeatedly *do*. You play like you practice. Put garbage in, you get garbage out. Not all relationships are good for you. And I'll bet you know the ones I'm talking about.

Some, in fact, are in need of sacrifice.

Give It Up

I walked on to play football at West Virginia University. Didn't start until my last two years. Had to work my way up from the bottom. So I received a lot of experience in trying to come out from under the radar. I was hungry to get noticed. Never stopped competing—*hard*—for playing time.

But as much as I wanted to catch touchdown passes on Saturday afternoons, as much as I wanted people to see what I could do, I was also eager to be as useful to God as I could possibly be. Wanted people to hear what I had to say. So I'd go to FCA meetings, church groups, looking for places where I could speak about my faith in God and what He'd done for me.

I remember thinking often, though, just how much more effective I could be if I were a big man on the depth chart, if my play was pulling down the kind of press coverage that made me a known figure in the community.

But that wasn't the way it was. I was just an ordinary guy. Nothing special. A uniform with a number and name on the back but pretty much just a body taking up space in the team picture. Middle row, third from left.

BOWDEN, Tommy.

You know what that really meant, though? It just meant that if I was going to be an effective witness for Christ, the school media guide wasn't going to do all the work for me. People wouldn't just naturally be flocking around to hang on every word of their hometown football superstar. I wouldn't be featured on the church sign out front as the guest speaker—the main attraction for Sunday night's service.

"Bring your friends, 7:00." Instead, I would have to step out of the shadows, out of the safety of anonymity, and share a message of faith that some people might not even care to hear.

The truth is, that's probably where you are today. Just an ordinary guy, an average Christian, asking, "Who wants to hear what somebody like me has to say?"

But I take you back to where this chapter began—back to the cross, the nails, the whip, the crown of thorns, Jesus' staggering walk down the Via Dolorosa, bloodied and beaten, enduring the mocking taunts of His torturers and killers— and I ask you: What are you not willing to sacrifice in order to tell other people about Him?

Is it the soft sofa of your comfort zone?

Is it the insecurity of not knowing what to say?

Is it the fear of coming off sounding holier than thou?

What is it?

And how confident do you feel, holding on to all these excuses, when you look into the eyes of the One who gave up everything—*everything*—to pay the blood debt that you owe, and I owe, and everybody on your street will owe if they don't receive His gift of grace with their personal faith and belief?

A well-done life will cost you a lot. Time. Approval. Lifestyle choices. Maybe even some friends along the way who'll just never seem able to understand what drives you. But while you're working at making all these necessary sacrifices to build a winning character, be sure you're never standing in the way of helping other people see what can give them the most victorious hope of all.

What you're willing to sacrifice in life will go a long way toward determining what God chooses to accomplish through you.

Final Call to Character

The year 2008 was advertised as the "year of the Tiger." We had just come off a nine-win season, narrowly losing to Auburn in an overtime thriller at the Chick-fil-A Bowl in Atlanta. Our fifth-year senior quarterback was set to return, one of sixteen total starters from the 2007 team, including a pair of star running backs as well as the entire defensive secondary. Preseason polls had placed us in the top ten nationally for the first time in my nine previous seasons at Clemson, and the expectations were high as a kite. The outlook for winning our first conference championship since 1991—the year when some hotshot team from Tallahassee had decided to join up and started hogging all the trophies—seemed well within our reach.

The schedule makers had conspired to make it hard on us, however, or at least to make us earn our bragging rights beginning with week one. Games against the likes of South Carolina State and the Citadel wouldn't come until after we'd faced second-year coach Nick Saban's Alabama squad on national television, opening weekend, Saturday night at the Georgia Dome. Feature matchup.

And we shanked it bad. We were never in the game. Sent a lot of our fans off to an early bedtime that night after amassing a grand total of zero rushing yards—our only touchdown coming on a C. J. Spiller ninety-six-yard kickoff return to open the second half. It was an embarrassing way to start the year, even if we *were* playing against a team that would eventually go undefeated throughout the regular season, earn the #1 ranking, and lose only to #2 Florida in the SEC championship game and to #7 Utah in the Sugar Bowl.

After that we did our best to rebound. That's what good teams do. And we truly seemed to be righting the ship over the next several weeks, building the foundation for what we hoped would become an eleven-game winning streak and a return to the overall title discussion—just when an underdog Maryland team came into Death Valley the last Saturday in September and rallied from behind in the fourth quarter to beat us 20–17.

Crushing.

I assure you, nobody could possibly have been any unhappier than I was, sitting at my desk on Monday morning, October 13, having watched not only our collapse against Maryland from two weeks before but also our flat performance in a 12–7 defeat on the road at Wake Forest the following Thursday, stamping our once hopeful dream of a special season with an average, disappointing 3–3 record.

That was *not* where I thought we'd be.

About 6:15 that morning Terry Don Phillips, our AD, knocked on the door to my office and asked if I had a minute to talk. I was actually sitting there doing my devotions, had my Bible open, spending some much-needed time in the Word before our regular 7:00 staff meeting. But obviously, an interruption like that took precedence over everything else at the moment, so I invited him in. Shut the door.

We had a professional conversation. Business-like. Nobody raised their voice or lost composure. But he did let me know he had some decisions to make (no surprise to me) and that he was considering some changes that affected me personally.

Perhaps immediately.

After a few minutes of talking, he got up, left the room, pulled the door behind him, and left me in there by myself. To think about it.

I remember bowing my head and praying, asking God for His help and wisdom. I remember picking up the phone and calling my father, getting his advice on how I might ought to proceed. I called my wife to let her know what was going on. I also called Steve Sloan, my friend and coaching mentor from my days at Duke, whose counsel I always sought on serious matters such as these. By the time I'd hung up the phone and prayed a little more, I knew what I had to do.

Before the sun had risen too hot on that otherwise typical fall morning in eastern South Carolina, the head football coaching position at Clemson University had become a head coaching vacancy. I had decided to do what seemed best for everyone involved. I wanted it to work, and I was still confident I could turn things around, like every time before. But . . .

I was stepping down.

It was over.

I did ask for the chance to talk with my team face-to-face before word got out. The AD said that'd be fine. I was able to come to the kind of agreements over contract clauses and so forth that need to be discussed and negotiated whenever a program changes hands like that, especially in midseason. But by 11:00 that morning—instead of being at work getting ready for practice and a big game against Georgia Tech the following weekend—I was back home.

And I picked up where I'd left off my devotions from earlier.

I really did.

That kind of situation may seem like a time for getting lost in your own thoughts, or calling people on the phone to help you process what had just happened—what had changed so dramatically in your life since you'd gone to bed the night before. I mean, obviously I was feeling the weight of it all in my heart and in my emotions. It wasn't like I had just driven home to make myself a sandwich, as though nothing had happened, like it was no big deal. But I knew this: more than I needed anything else right then, I needed God. I needed anchoring. And I believed the best way to do that was by staying true to what I'd committed to Him. Being in His Word. First above all.

I look back on that day now and, yeah, it was hard to see my coaching years at Clemson come to such a sudden and disappointing close, even knowing how those kinds of things can happen to anybody. (My father and Coach Paterno, for instance—the #1 and #2 winningest coaches in the history of college football—*both* of them were fired! How about that? I figure I'm in pretty good company.) But God used even that difficult experience to show me again just how strong He is— and just how secure *we* are when we offer our character up to Him to be shaped and molded by His hand.

I'm certainly not a solid enough man to be able to come home from having suddenly, abruptly lost my job of nine and a half years and calmly open my Bible back up to see what I'd missed from my devotions that morning—what I'd missed by having to break off my time with Him to plan my unexpected resignation speech at a televised press conference that afternoon.

But that's what God enables even His most ordinary men to do—men who are committed to letting Him establish their character on the solid ground of Scripture.

I had seen enough situations like these from the outside—even as an assistant, like when Pat Dye was fired while I was on staff at Auburn—that I knew how the script usually played out. It would be a hot story on ESPN and the national wires for a day or two. It'd be hard to avoid the media onslaught for a brief but explosive interval of time. Before the week was out, however, they'd have a new plan in motion, an interim coach in place, and the circus magic that is college football would've provided by then a much hotter, much juicier, much more captivating story line to take center stage. I was sure of that.

So I remember praying late that morning, sitting by myself at our boat dock down at the lake, scribbling out some notes of what I wanted to say both to my team and to the press and just asking God to help me endure the next twenty-four to forty-eight hours—after which I knew my life would go on, somehow, somewhere. I'd be able to put a big period at the end of what had turned out to be (on balance) a pretty impressive Plan A and start thinking ahead to the possibilities of a new and different Plan B.

And, boy, did He answer that prayer!

My phone starting ringing almost immediately. Within a week to ten days, I'd been asked to come speak at an FCA event during bowl week that winter in Mobile, Alabama.

Then another call—another bowl week appearance—this time in Tampa. Then a speaking engagement request for bowl week in Orlando. One after another. Things I'd never before had the time to pursue actively at this level of involvement— the kind of faith-based speaking I'd always wanted to do more and more of—God was now opening it up right in front of me, before I could even get used to being unemployed.

He also gave me some opportunities to do a little TV commentary for ESPN, the kind that's routinely offered to out-of-work or out-of-contention head coaches that the networks think can bring a firsthand perspective to their broadcasts. I enjoyed that a lot more than I expected. In fact, when the new year rolled around and I started trying to think of ways to keep myself busy, I approached ESPN myself to see if I might be able to do something on a more permanent basis with them going forward.

But just when that idea seemed to be drying up, the phone rang again—twice, in fact. One of the calls was from Raycom Sports, a broadcast programming company who was wanting to launch a live TV show covering ACC football. The second was from Fox Sports South, who was also starting up a new college football show, set to debut later that year.

So the one thing I'd tried to get hired onto at ESPN hadn't worked out. Going after that was *my* plan. But God's plan was to open the door for me to be part of *two* shows— neither of which even existed when I'd first started looking.

And as if that wasn't enough, I was soon approached about partnering with LifeWay Christian Resources in Nashville to become a regular speaker at their various ministry events, particularly through their men's ministry area. Seeing the opportunity to be involved in faith-based speaking on an ongoing basis to a national audience was more important to me than everything else put together. Who would have thought my path would take this kind of turn—so fast, so fulfilling? Not me.

I've been told when you're trying to spiritually analyze an event in your life: if you can explain it, God didn't do it. The definition of a miracle is when you watch something occur that cannot be explained any other way than that *God did it*—not you!

I know I could never have figured out how to locate two separate employment opportunities that played right into my skill set and my current situation. Nor was I smart enough to construct a faith-based speaking platform that would lay out a full slate of event opportunities as far as the eye could see. But by sitting tight, staying committed to God's Word, listening for Him in prayer, and expecting Him to keep me in His will, I was able to watch Him provide for me and my family—the way He *always* provides for those He's grooming in character.

Yes, character. It always comes back to character.

C-A-R-D-S character.

There's always a job for that somewhere.

So I want to encourage you today, if you're feeling left out of the opportunities to do what you feel capable of doing, if you're discouraged while looking for work that's not materializing yet, if you're not happy with where you are in life or the direction in which things seem to be going, try to spend this season working harder on your character than you are on your Rolodex. Invest in the kinds of character qualities that will pay off in whatever setting the Lord decides to put you. Spend each day dialing that moral compass of yours to true north. And then no matter *what* opportunity presents itself, you'll be ready to turn it into a winning proposition.

That's how the best guys do it.

Every Friday before a Saturday game—and usually again on Saturday morning—head coaches go over the game rotations with their staff. The average college football game includes about seventy plays on each side of the ball—seventy on offense, seventy on defense. But out of your eleven starters, you can't count on each of them playing every single down. They'll need a rest. You'll need to pace them. So you work out a rotation system before the game even begins. The individual assistants put together general guidelines for how much time certain starters will be on the field—every third series, for example, twenty plays in the first half, twenty-five plays in the second half, whatever the situation and opponent seem to call for.

But when I was on the sideline of a tight game, late in the fourth quarter, clock winding down, three points difference on the scoreboard, I'd better not look out there and see my second and third team on the field—I don't care *what* the rotation was drawn up to be. The game's on the line at that point. Every play from here on is critical. No way do I want my starters standing around on the sidelines with their helmets off, straightening their socks or getting their ankles retaped, taking water and trying to cool off. I want the guys in there that I know can win.

My *best guys*.

And it's the same way in the game of life. God will put His best guys out there. He will send in the ones who've shown a mature taste for "solid food," the ones whose "senses have been trained to distinguish between good and evil" (Heb. 5:14)—between good and better, between better and best.

Life calls for those guys. The best guys. Committed guys. Accountable guys. Responsible guys. Disciplined guys. Guys who are willing to sacrifice whatever it takes to be successful at what God Himself has called them to do.

Character guys.

So I challenge you today to join me in making that goal a part of every morning you're given the privilege of waking up to greet. Put your effort into building a wall of character that's strong enough to handle whatever life can dish out.

You may just be ordinary. Average. Commonplace. But nothing can keep you from becoming one of those "best guys" who *knows* how to win because you *know* what it takes.

It takes character.

Winning character.

HCSB
Take a
fresh look

Every word matters.

Every word of Scripture matters because every word is from God and for people. Because every word is from God, the HCSB uses words like Yahweh (Is. 42:8), Messiah (Luke 3:15), and slave (Rev. 1:1). And because every word of Scripture is for 21st century people, the HCSB replaces words like "Behold" with modern terms like "Look." For these reasons and others, Christians across the globe are taking a fresh look at the HCSB.

HCSB
Every Word Matters
HCSB.org